3-Minute
NIGHTTIME
PRAYERS
for
Teen Girls

3-Minute
NIGHTTIME
PRAYERS
for
Teen Girls

HILARY BERNSTEIN

BARBOUR
PUBLISHING

Published by Barbour Publishing, Inc., 1810 Barbour Drive, Uhrichsville, Ohio 44683, www.barbourbooks.com

Our mission is to inspire the world with the life-changing message of the Bible.

Printed in China.

When you lie down,
you will not be afraid;
when you lie down,
your sleep will be sweet.

PROVERBS 3:24 NIV

3 MINUTES TO A SWEET, PEACEFUL SLEEP IS RIGHT HERE.

If ever there was a time of needing a good night's rest, it's now. Every day, things scream for your attention: friends, school, family, social media, chores, activities, relationships, emotions. . . It's easy to get distracted from what really matters. Those distractions have a way of wearing you out and stealing your peace and joy so it's hard to fall asleep at night.

Life's busyness and distractions don't just threaten to rob your sleep; they make it harder to get close to your heavenly Father too. Yet He's the one who longs to bring you peace. He's the one who will make your sleep sweet.

During this time when everything in your life seems so topsy-turvy and uncertain, this book can help you refocus on our Lord and His Word. I pray it will quiet your heart, fill you with peace, and bring restful nights of sweet sleep.

Sweet dreams!
Hilary Bernstein

JESUS LOVES ME

I pray that you, being rooted and established in love, may have power, together with all the Lord's holy people, to grasp how wide and long and high and deep is the love of Christ, and to know this love that surpasses knowledge—that you may be filled to the measure of all the fullness of God.

Ephesians 3:17–19 NIV

Father God, Your love is amazing. And Jesus' love for me is beyond what I can even wrap my brain around. I don't need to do anything on my own to earn that love. All I need is to believe in Him and accept His love as a beautiful gift. Day by day, moment by moment, please give me power to begin to grasp how wide and long and high and deep Christ's love is for me. It can transform every part of my life! In Jesus' name I pray, amen.

Think about it!
What makes God's love so special?

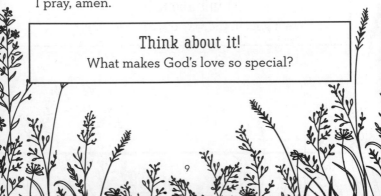

STOP STRIVING

"Be still, and know that I am God."
PSALM 46:10 ESV

Father, I come to You weighed down by my busyness. So much is going on in my life, and I feel like I'm cramming so much into my days. I know I don't have to do all the things to make You love me. In fact, Your Word tells me to be still and know You are God. That means I need to stop striving. I admit it feels almost impossible to be still. It's hard to not strive, and it feels like everything in this world is so far from being still. Yet tonight, as I draw close to You, I choose to quiet my heart. I want to take this time to be still with You. In this quiet place, please help me to know You are God. In Jesus' name I pray, amen.

Think about it!
What gets in the way of you being still?

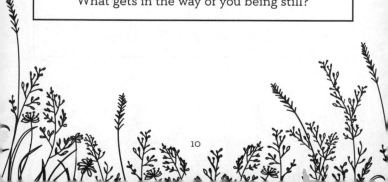

NO WORRIES

Humble yourselves, therefore, under God's mighty hand, that he may lift you up in due time. Cast all your anxiety on him because he cares for you.

1 PETER 5:6–7 NIV

Father, I'm so glad You love me and that I matter to You. And I'm so thankful I can tell You all of my cares and worries. I know You'll listen to me and help. So many things feel like burdens right now. They're weighing me down. But I choose to surrender them to You. I know I can't handle all that I'm facing and feeling, but I know You can. You're mighty enough to do more than I can even imagine. I trust You'll work out all the details. When I'm tempted to feel anxious, please replace all of my worry with peace. Please help me trust You completely and rest in that trust. In Jesus' name I pray, amen.

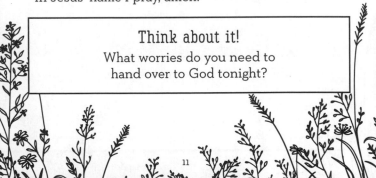

Think about it!
What worries do you need to hand over to God tonight?

MORE THAN SKIN DEEP

But the LORD said to Samuel, "Do not consider his appearance or his height, for I have rejected him. The LORD does not look at the things people look at. People look at the outward appearance, but the LORD looks at the heart."

1 SAMUEL 16:7 NIV

Father God, it's hard to *not* focus on my appearance. I don't always like what I see, even though You created me and You see what's inside of me. It's also really hard to not judge other people by what they look like. I know I shouldn't, but I do. Please help me see what's really inside others so I can make wise choices about my friends. Please open my eyes to see people who need You—and help me to reach out to them. Please help me look deeper than just the surface level. In Jesus' name I pray, amen.

Think about it!
How can you do a better job of loving the person you see in the mirror?

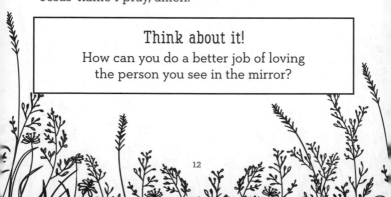

TOMORROW

Yet you do not know what your life will be like tomorrow. You are just a vapor that appears for a little while and then vanishes away.

JAMES 4:14 NASB

Lord, it's hard for me to remember that the worries and troubles of today won't last forever. I don't know what tomorrow will hold. But I'm choosing to trust You. As much as I wonder what will happen tomorrow—or next week or next month or next year—I don't have to worry. I know You're in control, and You have a wonderful plan. Even if it doesn't always feel like it, life is so short. Please help me make the most of every day. Especially my not-so-great days! Instead of getting discouraged or frustrated when things don't go my way, please help me to see You at work and trust You more and more. In Jesus' name I pray, amen.

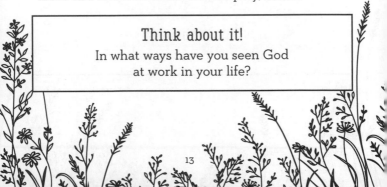

Think about it!
In what ways have you seen God
at work in your life?

SPEAK UP!

Speak up for those who cannot speak for themselves, for the rights of all who are destitute. Speak up and judge fairly; defend the rights of the poor and needy.

PROVERBS 31:8–9 NIV

Father God, thank You for giving me a voice! You've given me thoughts and words not only to express my feelings but also to speak up for others. Please use me to help other people, even if it seems awkward or uncomfortable. Please work on my heart so I have more compassion. Open my eyes so I can see who needs help. I pray I'll be a kind friend to other teens who are left out. Please help me include outsiders and treat everyone with kindness, no matter what. I'm trusting that You'll use me in a big way in someone else's life. In Jesus' name I pray, amen.

Think about it!
Why is it so hard to speak up?

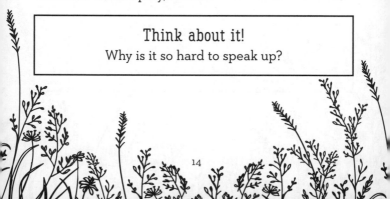

MY MOUTH AND MY HEART

*If you confess with your mouth Jesus as Lord, and
believe in your heart that God raised Him from
the dead, you will be saved; for with the heart a
person believes, resulting in righteousness, and
with the mouth he confesses, resulting in salvation.*
ROMANS 10:9–10 NASB

Jesus, I confess that You are Lord! I truly believe in my
heart of hearts that God raised You from the dead and
that You're living right now. Thank You for saving me
when I confessed in faith that You're my Lord. Thank
You that, as I believe in You, You make me right with
You. Being saved and being made right—salvation and
righteousness—are such huge things I could never
accomplish on my own. You are so very good! In Your
name I pray, amen.

Think about it!
What does it really mean to be saved
and made right with the Lord?

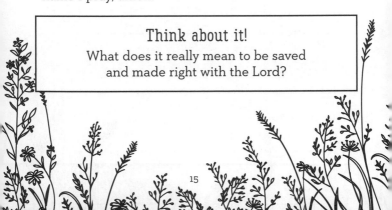

15

A LIFE OF KINDNESS

*Whoever pursues righteousness and kindness
will find life, righteousness, and honor.*
PROVERBS 21:21 ESV

Heavenly Father, it's so interesting that, just like believers should be known for their love, if I pursue kindness—a very loving trait—I'll find life. I pray that I'll seek and find a life of love and kindness. I want to be right in Your eyes. I want to bring kindness to others. I'm definitely happy to find righteousness and honor along the way. But instead of only focusing on those rewards, I'd rather concentrate on living a life that pleases You and blesses the people You bring across my path. I admit that some days I'd rather not be very righteous or kind at all. But deep down, I want to do all these things for Your glory, Lord! In Jesus' name I pray, amen.

Think about it!
Why is it important to be kind to others?

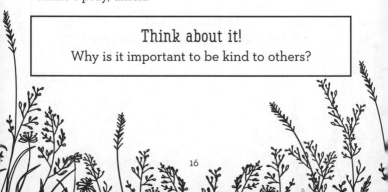

SAFE AND PROTECTED

*I love you, O LORD, my strength. The LORD is
my rock and my fortress and my deliverer, my
God, my rock, in whom I take refuge, my shield,
and the horn of my salvation, my stronghold.
I call upon the LORD, who is worthy to be
praised, and I am saved from my enemies.*
PSALM 18:1–3 ESV

O Lord, I love You! What a relief to know that You
are my strength, my rock, my fortress. Whenever I'm
in trouble, You come to my rescue. Even when my
enemies verbally or physically threaten me, I know
You'll save me. You're my protector, and I praise You!
I'm thankful I can put my trust in You and call upon
You at any time. As I fall asleep tonight, help me rest
peacefully, knowing You care about me and shield
me, moment by moment. In Jesus' name I pray, amen.

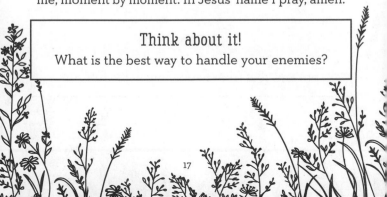

Think about it!
What is the best way to handle your enemies?

A GOOD WORK

*For I am confident of this very thing, that
He who began a good work in you will
perfect it until the day of Christ Jesus.*

PHILIPPIANS 1:6 NASB

Father, sometimes I look at my life and it doesn't feel like there are many good things in it. My relationships are confusing. Life feels like a complete mess and not at all how I wish it was. But I trust You. I'm overwhelmed that You've begun a good work in me. And by faith, I know You'll keep working until it's complete. I don't have to worry about perfecting Your work on my own because You're in control. And You'll handle it! Please help me to not get in Your way. Open my eyes so I can see some of the good works You're accomplishing in me and through me. In Jesus' name I pray, amen.

Think about it!

Do you ever get in God's way? How can you prevent that from happening in the future?

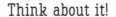

18

PLEASE FORGIVE ME

*I do not understand what I do. For what I want
to do I do not do, but what I hate I do.*

ROMANS 7:15 NIV

Father, I have sinned against You—and I really, really
regret it. I wish it wasn't so easy to sin. I wish I could
obey You more. I wish I could make good decisions.
Tomorrow, please help me honor You moment by
moment in what I think, say, and do. Please help me
live a righteous life—not in a holier-than-thou, judg-
mental sort of way toward my friends and family. But
in the hidden places of my heart, please help me live
the kind of life that reflects You as my Lord. I want to
be authentic and live for You, not for myself. In Jesus'
name I pray, amen.

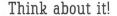

Think about it!
Why is our behavior so important?
Does it really affect others *that* much?

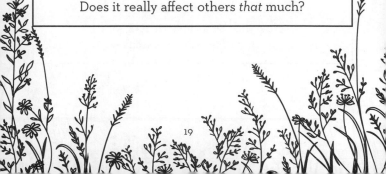

BELIEVE AND LOVE

This is his command: to believe in the name of his Son, Jesus Christ, and to love one another as he commanded us. The one who keeps God's commands lives in him, and he in them. And this is how we know that he lives in us: We know it by the Spirit he gave us.

1 JOHN 3:23–24 NIV

Lord, I believe in Your name. I want to do what You've commanded. You lived a life of love and I want to do the same. Please help Your love be a light in the way I treat others. When I need to deal with hard-to-love people, please help me choose to show them kindness and compassion. Thank You for Your love—it changed my life for eternity! Thank You, also, for Your Spirit and for the way He is proof that You live in me. In Your name I pray, amen.

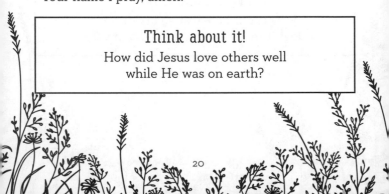

Think about it!
How did Jesus love others well
while He was on earth?

IN GOD I TRUST

Some trust in chariots and some in horses,
but we trust in the name of the LORD our God.
PSALM 20:7 ESV

Father, when I look around, I see people trusting in all sorts of things—money, power, grades, friends, clothing, social media likes, and themselves. But why trust in any of that? What can those things do? If they aren't fleeting—and so many of them are—they're powerless. I don't want to trust in the things of this world. I don't want to get caught up in obsessing over what's temporary. And I certainly don't want to trust in myself. But I trust *You.* I trust that You have all power and authority. Help me to fully rest in You when I'm tempted to shift my eyes and attention to myself or trivial things. Thank You for being trustworthy! In Jesus' name I pray, amen.

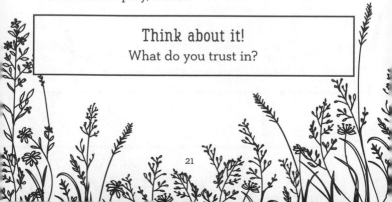

Think about it!
What do you trust in?

HERE I AM!

Then I heard the voice of the Lord saying, "Whom shall I send? And who will go for us?" And I said, "Here am I. Send me!"
ISAIAH 6:8 NIV

Father, You are awesome. Before anything was, You were. You spoke everything into existence. And You had—*and still have*—a plan for everything and everyone. Even me. Sometimes I wonder if You can ever use me to do great things for You. But as long as I listen to Your direction and obey, You can and will use me. That's amazing! Please give me strength and courage to step out and do Your work. When there's fear in my heart, replace it with courage. When I doubt what I should do, please give me clarity. When I'm tempted to stick to what's comfortable, help me choose obedience. Here I am. Send me. In Jesus' name I pray, amen.

Think about it!
What are the Lord's plans for your future?
Have you asked Him about it?

NO DRIFTING

We must pay the most careful attention, therefore, to what we have heard, so that we do not drift away.

HEBREWS 2:1 NIV

Father God, I'm so glad I've heard Your truth. Not only have I heard it, but I fully believe it and want to obey it! I want to follow You. I don't want to drift away. Even when I feel pushed and pulled to be more like the world, I want to be more like You. I don't want to fall into the trap of doing things to fit in with my friends. And I don't want to do what's popular if it doesn't line up with Your truth. Please help me to bravely live for You. Keep me close to You. Show me what Your good, pleasing, and perfect will is for my life. In Jesus' name I pray, amen.

Think about it!
What worldly "traps" do you face every day?

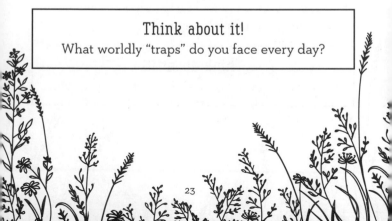

23

ALL MY HEART

*Trust in the LORD with all your heart and
do not lean on your own understanding.
In all your ways acknowledge Him, and
He will make your paths straight.*

PROVERBS 3:5–6 NASB

Father, when I tell You that I struggle with trusting in myself, it comes as no surprise to You. Honestly, I do lean on my own understanding. I try to figure things out on my own. I try to set my own course and live my way. But, Lord, I need You. I need to trust You. I need to lean on Your understanding. I want to acknowledge You in all of my ways because You are the living God. It's a bonus that You'll make my paths straight and help make sense of my life. Please help me to stop trying to direct my own life and instead live out my belief in You. In Jesus' name I pray, amen.

Think about it!
Why is it so hard to give God control of your life?

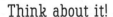

WEIGHED DOWN

But You, O LORD, are a shield about me, my glory, and the One who lifts my head. I was crying to the LORD with my voice, and He answered me from His holy mountain.

PSALM 3:3–4 NASB

Father, I come to You weighed down by life. I am sad and discouraged. You know the details. You know what burdens my heart. You know what I can't get off my mind. Even in all my despair and frustration, I can rest in You. You're my shield of protection. You and You alone are my glory—my excellence! You lift my head when it's heavy with tears and exhaustion. I am so thankful I can come to You for comfort. I praise You for Your goodness and Your never-ending love for me. Thank You for listening to my prayers and answering them. I love You so very much. In Jesus' name I pray, amen.

Think about it!
What burdens weigh heavy on your heart tonight? Give them to God!

WHAT SHOULD I WEAR?

"Why are you worried about clothing? Observe how the lilies of the field grow; they do not toil nor do they spin, yet I say to you that not even Solomon in all his glory clothed himself like one of these. But if God so clothes the grass of the field, which is alive today and tomorrow is thrown into the furnace, will He not much more clothe you?"

MATTHEW 6:28–30 NASB

Father, Jesus promised that I don't have to worry about the clothing I wear. That is so different than the focus of the world. But just like You clothe the lilies of the field so beautifully, You'll clothe me too. Please help me notice the wonderful ways You always provide—ways that I don't have to worry about or consider. Thank You, Lord! You are so, so good to me! In Jesus' name I pray, amen.

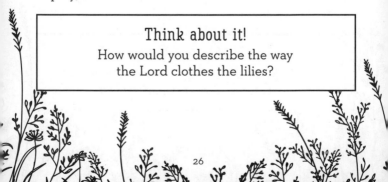

Think about it!
How would you describe the way
the Lord clothes the lilies?

CHOSEN BY YOU

He predestined us to adoption as sons through Jesus Christ to Himself, according to the kind intention of His will, to the praise of the glory of His grace, which He freely bestowed on us in the Beloved.
EPHESIANS 1:5–6 NASB

Father, I admit that I don't always understand Your plan for me. But even when I can't understand it, I can still appreciate it. So tonight, I thank You for choosing to adopt me. You could choose absolutely anyone in the world, so to know that You've chosen *me* is amazing! I praise You. Thank You for Your grace, given so generously through Jesus. I know I don't deserve it; but even so, I pray I might start living my life in a way that is worthy of You and Your gift. In Jesus' name I pray, amen.

Think about it!
How does it feel knowing God chose you?

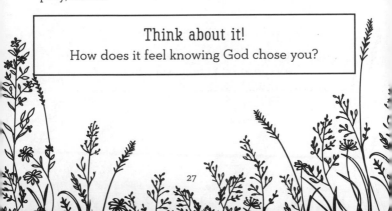

WATCH YOURSELF!

Brothers and sisters, if someone is caught in a sin, you who live by the Spirit should restore that person gently. But watch yourselves, or you also may be tempted.

GALATIANS 6:1 NIV

Father, I found out that one of my friends is making some very bad choices. The thing is, I don't know if my friend is even sorry. It almost seems like she is enjoying the sin. I'm upset by it—and I don't want to follow the same path. Could You please help me? I'd like to follow Your Word and try to gently help my friend recognize her bad choices. But I'm worried I might be tempted in the process. Please keep me from falling into the same sin. I love You and want to do what's right in Your eyes. In Jesus' name I pray, amen.

Think about it!

What can you say to a friend who's making all the wrong choices for her life?

BULLIED

But the salvation of the righteous is from the LORD; He is their strength in time of trouble. The LORD helps them and delivers them; He delivers them from the wicked and saves them, because they take refuge in Him.

PSALM 37:39–40 NASB

Father God, the bullies in my life are awful! They do and say such horrible things. My heart feels broken, and my confidence is shattered. Please help me remember that You don't see me the same way they do—and most people don't see me that way either. Please be my strength when I don't have any. When I'm in danger, please rescue me. Keep me safe. Bring something good out of this bad situation. Help me shine Your light even when I feel like I can't. Instead of seeking revenge, please help me treat my enemies with undeserved love, just like Jesus did. In His name I pray, amen.

Think about it!
Why should you show God's love and light to a bully?

GOTTA HAVE FAITH

*Faith is confidence in what we hope for and
assurance about what we do not see.*
HEBREWS 11:1 NIV

Father God, I admit that sometimes it doesn't seem
like You're real. When You seem so quiet, it's hard to
remember that You're the living God. I want to believe
in You. I want to worship You. Please help me keep
my faith—and to grow it even stronger! Even when I
don't feel like You're there, please help me remember
that faith is not a feeling, and the truth of Your existence doesn't depend on whether I can see or feel or
hear You. You are there. . .always. You are real, living,
and at work in the world today. Thank You for loving
me even when I'm tempted to doubt You. In Jesus'
name I pray, amen.

Think about it!
When does it feel like God is far away?
When does it feel like He's very close?

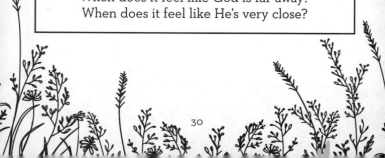

SEEK PEACE AND PURSUE IT

Whoever of you loves life and desires to see many good days, keep your tongue from evil and your lips from telling lies. Turn from evil and do good; seek peace and pursue it.

PSALM 34:12–14 NIV

Heavenly Father, it's tough to live in peace with everyone. But even when conflict is all around me, I want to choose peace. I want to do good. I want to let Your light shine through my life. When people are stressed and worried, please help me be a peaceful influence. In the heat of the moment, help me to remember that the words I choose have influence and power. I pray You'll use me and my words to calm people down in a gentle way. I don't ever want to add to conflict by what I say or do. Please use me as a peacemaker. In Jesus' name I pray, amen.

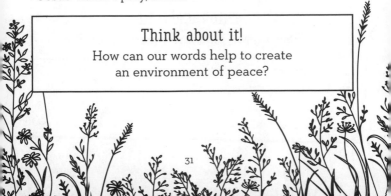

Think about it!
How can our words help to create an environment of peace?

DIFFERENT THAN THE WORLD

*But Noah found favor in the eyes of
the LORD. . . . And Noah did all that
the LORD had commanded him.*

GENESIS 6:8; 7:5 ESV

Lord, You have such a wonderful way of not only knowing Your children but also caring for them. You've proven this time and again in my life and also in Your Word through people like Noah. Even though Noah lived in a wicked world, he still honored and obeyed You. He did everything You told him to do, no matter how others reacted. Just like Noah, I often feel like I'm living in a wicked world. And even if my obedience to You makes me an easy target, I'll obey anyway. I trust You and only You. I love You and want to honor You every day of my life. In Jesus' name I pray, amen.

Think about it!
How are you different from the world?

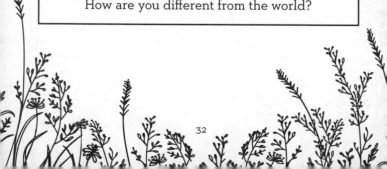

A LIVING HOPE

*Praise be to the God and Father of our Lord
Jesus Christ! In his great mercy he has given
us new birth into a living hope through the
resurrection of Jesus Christ from the dead, and
into an inheritance that can never perish, spoil
or fade. This inheritance is kept in heaven for
you, who through faith are shielded by God's
power until the coming of the salvation that
is ready to be revealed in the last time.*

1 PETER 1:3–5 NIV

Father, thank You for Your mercy that I don't deserve.
Thank You for hope that is real and living. I look forward to what's waiting for me in heaven. I'm thankful
that You shield me with Your power and guarantee
my future. I praise You for the way You care for me
today and will continue to care for me forever. In
Jesus' name I pray, amen.

Think about it!

What do you imagine heaven will be like?

GUARD YOUR HEART!

*Above all else, guard your heart, for
everything you do flows from it.*
PROVERBS 4:23 NIV

God, I know my heart is an important part of me that guides my thoughts and decisions. And often, culture tells me to follow my heart. But honestly, I don't really know what that means. My feelings seem to be all over the place—every day they seem to change, even moment by moment. Some days it feels like I'm on a wild roller coaster ride. Instead of trusting my ever-changing feelings, help me guard my heart more carefully. Please help me keep bad influences out and cling to the good influences that please You. Give me wisdom, Father, to know what needs to stay in my heart—and what things need to go. In Jesus' name I pray, amen.

Think about it!
What are some good influences you should cling to?

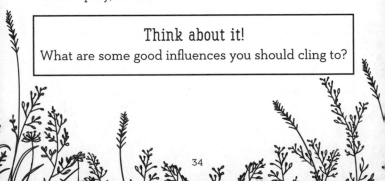

GET WELL SOON

Have mercy on me, LORD, for I am faint;
heal me, LORD, for my bones are in agony.
PSALM 6:2 NIV

Father, I haven't been feeling very well lately. And it's starting to affect my attitude. I feel icky on the inside, and it's beginning to show in my mood and how I treat others. I know everything happens for a reason. But honestly, Father, I don't want to feel this way! Please heal me. Restore my health and help me feel better. When I'm tempted to worry about what's wrong, please fill me with Your peace. When I want to complain about how I feel, remind me of everything that's good in my life. Help me to get plenty of rest so I can feel like myself again. In Jesus' name I pray, amen.

Think about it!

Is it really possible to have a good attitude when you're not feeling well? Why or why not?

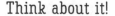

BECOMING A DO-GOODER

And let us not grow weary of doing good, for in due season we will reap, if we do not give up.
GALATIANS 6:9 ESV

Father God, sometimes it feels like I try so hard to do good things—to make life better for other people, to do my very best, to be a good example of what it's like to follow You. But all of that goodness wears me out. I get tired. But even when I'm feeling weary, I trust You'll give me the strength to keep going. I don't want to be a quitter. And I really don't want to stop doing good things. Please help me see even just a tiny result of what my good deeds are accomplishing for You in the people around me. I love You, and I want to serve You with my whole life. In Jesus' name I pray, amen.

Think about it!

Why is doing good so exhausting at times?
What can you do to keep the exhaustion at bay?

NOT MY OWN

Do you not know that your bodies are temples of the Holy Spirit, who is in you, whom you have received from God? You are not your own; you were bought at a price. Therefore honor God with your bodies.

1 CORINTHIANS 6:19–20 NIV

Father, in today's world, impurity is everywhere. From things people say to things people do, purity has become something foreign. Yet, as strange as purity seems today, Your truth hasn't changed. My body is a temple of the Holy Spirit and Your Spirit is living inside of me. As a temple of Your Holy Spirit, I need to live like it. I'm not my own! And so I need to honor You with my body. Please help me to remember I was bought at a huge price. I want to honor Christ's sacrifice with my purity. In Jesus' name I pray, amen.

Think about it!
What does it mean that your body
is a temple of the Holy Spirit?

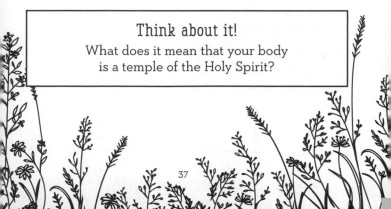

WALKING THE WALK

Therefore as you have received Christ Jesus the Lord, so walk in Him, having been firmly rooted and now being built up in Him and established in your faith, just as you were instructed, and overflowing with gratitude.

COLOSSIANS 2:6–7 NASB

Father, thank You for Jesus. Thank You for His love for me. I believe He is Your Son, who led a perfect life then died a cruel death on the cross. His death paid for my sins. Because I believe He is the only way, the only truth, and the only life, I boldly come to You through Him. He has forgiven me of my sins. I pray that with this new life and forgiveness, I would be rooted and built up in Him. May the things I think, say, and do be filled with faith and devotion to You. In Jesus' name I pray, amen.

Think about it!
What does it mean to walk in Christ?

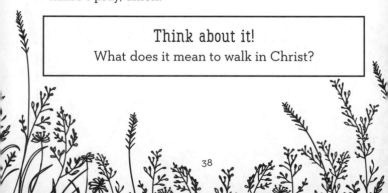

TOGETHER

Only let your manner of life be worthy of the gospel of Christ, so that whether I come and see you or am absent, I may hear of you that you are standing firm in one spirit, with one mind striving side by side for the faith of the gospel, and not frightened in anything by your opponents. This is a clear sign to them of their destruction, but of your salvation, and that from God.

PHILIPPIANS 1:27–28 ESV

Lord, I pray that my life would be joined to the lives of other believers. Please bless me with good relationships—mentors and friends who can help keep me close to You and who also love You. I pray that through fellowship we can encourage one another to stand firm for the truth of the gospel. Thank You that I never have to walk alone. In Your name I pray, amen.

Think about it!
Who are the best Christian mentors and friends in your life right now?

WHAT IS TRUTH?

Jesus answered, "You say correctly that I am a king. For this I have been born, and for this I have come into the world, to testify to the truth. Everyone who is of the truth hears My voice." Pilate said to Him, "What is truth?"

JOHN 18:37–38 NASB

Lord, the world is a confusing place. There's so much noise with people sharing their ideas of right and wrong. I hear many contradicting opinions, and nothing seems to make sense. I pray that I can know and understand Your truth. I want it to guide my life. I want it to transform my choices and the way I think and live. Thank You that Your Word is true. Thank You that Jesus is the way, the truth, and the life. In His name I pray, amen.

Think about it!

With all the confusion in the world, how can you tell what's truth and what's not?

TRUST

Trust in the LORD and do good; dwell in the land and cultivate faithfulness. Delight yourself in the LORD; and He will give you the desires of your heart.
PSALM 37:3–4 NASB

Father God, the thought of delighting myself in You is special. I can completely enjoy You—being with You and getting to know You better. As I delight in You more and more, my trust in You grows. And trusting in You adds so much peace to my life. I don't have to worry. Instead, I get to rest in the fact that You are God. As I trust in You and delight myself in You, You shower me with more blessings than I can count! Shape the desires of my heart, Father. I am so grateful that I can trust You. In Jesus' name I pray, amen.

Think about it!
What are the desires of your heart?
Do they align with God's will for your life?

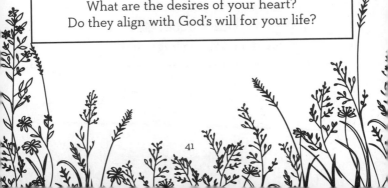

AFRAID AND DISCOURAGED?
OR STRONG AND COURAGEOUS?

*"Have I not commanded you? Be strong
and courageous. Do not be afraid; do not
be discouraged, for the LORD your God
will be with you wherever you go."*

JOSHUA 1:9 NIV

Father, I'm so thankful I can trust You. I'm thankful
You're in control. But honestly, Lord? . . . I'm scared. I
don't want to do what I must do. I don't feel brave at
all. In fact, I'm so nervous that I just want to hide. But
I know I need to be brave. And I need to remember
what's true: You're with me wherever I go. Because
You're with me, I don't ever have to be afraid or discouraged. Through You, I can be a courageous girl. I
trust You'll give me just what I need when I need it,
Lord. In Jesus' name I pray, amen.

Think about it!

Where does your courage come from?

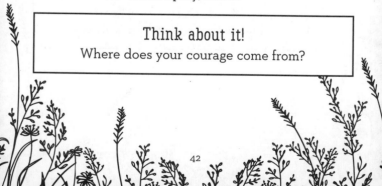

PERFECT LOVE

The LORD will keep you from all harm—he will watch over your life; the LORD will watch over your coming and going both now and forevermore.
PSALM 121:7–8 NIV

Father, it's comforting to know You'll keep me from harm. Tonight, I can go to sleep in peace because You're watching over my life—now and forever. You love me with a perfect love that is beyond my understanding. But knowing that You watch over me and protect me is just part of the proof of Your love. When I'm feeling anxious, please remind me of Your love and protection. Help me to walk confidently through each day, trusting that You are with me and *for* me. Rather than being overcome by fear, I want to experience the peace of Your love and confidence that nothing in this world can take away. Thank You. In Jesus' name I pray, amen.

Think about it!
What makes you feel perfectly loved and safe?

LEARNING TO TAKE ADVICE

"Hear instruction and be wise, and do not neglect it."
PROVERBS 8:33 ESV

Father, I admit that sometimes (okay—*most* times) I want things my way. I know what I want to do, and then I want to do it. I also think I know what's best for me. But truthfully? . . . I don't always know what's best. It can be really hard to accept the fact that other people can help point me in the right direction. If others have my best interests at heart, please help me to listen to their advice and then make a wise decision. Help me to remember that if someone's advice aligns with Your truth, Lord, then it's the right way to go. Whatever I choose, though, may my decisions always glorify and honor You. In Jesus' name I pray, amen.

Think about it!
What's the best advice you've ever received?

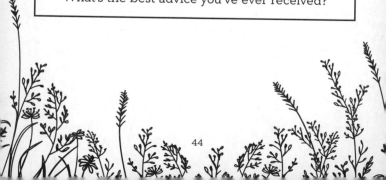

WHO AM I?

When I look at your heavens, the work of your fingers, the moon and the stars, which you have set in place, what is man that you are mindful of him, and the son of man that you care for him?

PSALM 8:3-4 ESV

Creator, I am in awe of You. You created everything! When I look around and see the sunrise and sunset, it's clear that You are the ultimate artist. When I gaze at the moon and stars at night and think about how small I am and how humongous the universe is, I'm amazed. It's mind-boggling to think of how You created humans so intricately and uniquely—and You know the hearts and minds of every single one of us. No one escapes Your notice! Every day You care for me so wonderfully. Thank You! In Jesus' name I pray, amen.

Think about it!
What is your favorite part of God's creation and why?

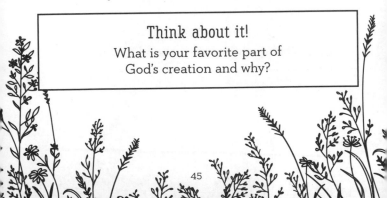

FRIENDS FOREVER

The friendship of the LORD is for those who fear him, and he makes known to them his covenant.

PSALM 25:14 ESV

Lord, sometimes I feel lonely. It doesn't seem like I have any true friends. When I feel loved and included, life is great; and I'm sent crashing down whenever I feel left out. In times like these, remind me that You are my friend. In fact, You're my *best* friend. You make good on every one of Your promises to me—and I'm grateful. Even though I don't always feel like I can measure up and be the kind of friend You deserve, Lord, I'm in awe of You. And in my awe, I respect Your power as well. I recognize who You are and am amazed You'd bother to be my friend. Thank You for Your love and kindness! In Jesus' name I pray, amen.

Think about it!
What qualities make a good friend?

YOUR LITTLE LAMB

*"I am the good shepherd; I know my sheep
and my sheep know me—just as the Father
knows me and I know the Father—and
I lay down my life for the sheep."*

JOHN 10:14-15 NIV

Lord, when I think of sheep, I picture cute fluffy creatures. But all the cuteness aside, sheep are pretty dumb. They wander off and get themselves into trouble. They need someone to lead them and guide them—to keep them safe from danger. They know their shepherd's voice and listen only to him. Just like those sweet but naive sheep, I need You to lead me and guide me too. I want to know Your voice. Thank You for caring for me, Good Shepherd. Because of You, I don't lack a single thing. And I'm so thankful. In Your name I pray, amen.

Think about it!
In what ways are humans like sheep
in need of a good shepherd?

47

MORE AND MORE

As for other matters, brothers and sisters, we instructed you how to live in order to please God, as in fact you are living. Now we ask you and urge you in the Lord Jesus to do this more and more.

1 THESSALONIANS 4:1 NIV

Lord, it's so tempting to live for myself every day. Looking for pleasure or trying to live for the moment seems really appealing. Yet, what I need to do—what's *better* to do—is to live in a way that will please You. Deep down I want to please You. I know the difference between right and wrong, good and bad. Just because I know what I should do doesn't mean it's always easy to do the right thing. Please speak to my conscience when I'm tempted to sin and wander from Your purpose and plan for me. Thank You, Father. In Jesus' name I pray, amen.

Think about it!
What can help you to get back on the right path when you begin to wander away from God's plan?

UNWORTHY. . .BUT GRATEFUL

*In him we have redemption through his blood,
the forgiveness of sins, in accordance with the
riches of God's grace that he lavished on us.*
Ephesians 1:7–8 niv

Jesus, You are perfect; and I, on the other hand, am not. But You love me anyway—despite my imperfection. And, even more wonderful, You do *so much more* than love me! You gave Your very life for me so I could be brought into a relationship with You. You bought me at a price. You've forgiven me of my sins. I have a lot of them, and You know every single one, yet You *still* forgive me. As if that isn't enough, You lavish me with undeserved blessings. I'm unworthy, but so very thankful. In Your name I pray, amen.

Think about it!
What has Jesus done for you?

WHITE AS SNOW

*"Come now, let us settle the matter," says the
LORD. "Though your sins are like scarlet, they
shall be as white as snow; though they are
red as crimson, they shall be like wool."*

ISAIAH 1:18 NIV

Lord Jesus, I am so thankful that the Bible is filled with
such vivid word pictures. My sins *are* like scarlet. I'm
guilty; and it's like my sin has stained me with bright
red paint. But the stains aren't permanent because
You've made it possible for my sins to be erased. Your
forgiveness washes me and turns me into a brand-
new creation. Through Your sacrifice, I'm clean. In
Your eyes, my crimson stain is gone, and I've become
white as snow. You've saved me. My guilt and shame
are gone. I can't thank You enough for Your amazing
gift. You are so good to me! In Your name I pray, amen.

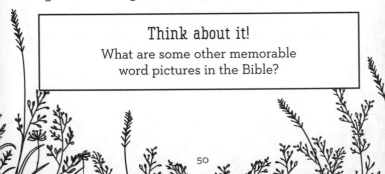

Think about it!
What are some other memorable
word pictures in the Bible?

MY HEART AT PEACE

A heart at peace gives life to the
body, but envy rots the bones.
PROVERBS 14:30 NIV

Father God, I desire peace. I know You're a peace giver—in fact, peace comes naturally when I'm living in step with Your Holy Spirit. When my heart is calm and resting in You, I feel more alive. I'm happy and content with what I have. And when I'm not at peace? Ew. So often, jealousy and envy rob my peace and distract me from all You've given me. I look and see what other people have and wonder why it can't be mine. The truth is, though, You've provided what's best for me. And You know *exactly* what I need, Father. Please help me learn how to be content in any circumstance so I can experience Your true peace. In Jesus' name I pray, amen.

Think about it!
When do you feel most content and at peace?

SUCH A TIME AS THIS

*"And who knows whether you have not come
to the kingdom for such a time as this?"*
ESTHER 4:14 ESV

Father, so often, I feel like time is going so slow. I know I should appreciate where I am right now and enjoy the moment. Amazingly, You've chosen this exact time and place in history for me. You know this is where I should be, right here and now. Please help me remember this when I find myself wishing the minutes and days away. Sometimes—*many* times—I'd rather fast-forward. What will I be like as a grown woman? Where will I work? Will I get married or have children? Where will I live? I have so many questions, and I'd love to know the answers. But for now, I will wait for You and Your perfect timing. In my waiting, help me enjoy all Your daily gifts. In Jesus' name I pray, amen.

Think about it!
What can you do to help yourself remember
to enjoy the moments each day brings?

UNCHANGING

Every good and perfect gift is from above, coming down from the Father of the heavenly lights, who does not change like shifting shadows.
JAMES 1:17 NIV

Father, it's amazing that You never change. You are who You say You are—today, tomorrow, and forever. You are my rock, my firm foundation. Everything in this world feels like it shifts and changes. But not You—You stay the same. You never move. You never leave me. Thank You for being a constant companion. Thank You for being the one I can completely trust. You know just what I need and when I need it—and You are a generous giver. Every single good and perfect gift comes from You. Thank You for being so good to me! I love You. In Jesus' name I pray, amen.

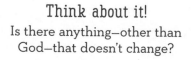

Think about it!
Is there anything—other than God—that doesn't change?

MAKING LIFE BETTER

The memory of the righteous is a blessing,
but the name of the wicked will rot.
PROVERBS 10:7 ESV

God, sometimes it's hard to keep in mind that even the little things I say or do leave an impression on others. In fact, how I treat people now will affect the way they'll remember me in the future. I want people to smile when they think of me. I don't want anyone to think negatively when I come to mind. Please help me to bless the lives of others, just by being myself. I pray that tomorrow You'll use me to make someone's day better. Please help me be an encouragement and let my life reflect Your love. I love You. It's such a privilege to represent You right where I am. In Jesus' name I pray, amen.

Think about it!
What are some words that others might use to describe you? *Funny, kind, smart. . . ?*

FOLLOWING HIS LEAD

I will praise the LORD, who counsels me;
even at night my heart instructs me. I keep
my eyes always on the LORD. With him at
my right hand, I will not be shaken.

PSALM 16:7–8 NIV

Lord, You are so good to me—especially in the way You lovingly and gently guide me. Please help me listen to You and then obey. Help me keep my eyes on You and not get distracted by worldly things. It's hard to not chase after my wants. Please help me to choose what's right in Your eyes, Father. I'd love my days to feel steady and sure; and if I follow You closely, I know I won't be shaken. Thank You for counseling me. I'll gladly welcome it, even when what You ask me to do is different than what I'd planned. I want to follow Your lead. In Jesus' name I pray, amen.

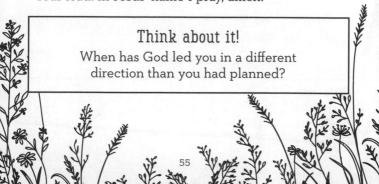

Think about it!
When has God led you in a different
direction than you had planned?

TO HAVE A FRIEND IS TO BE A FRIEND

One who has unreliable friends soon comes to ruin,
but there is a friend who sticks closer than a brother.
PROVERBS 18:24 NIV

Lord, Your Word says that Jesus is a friend who sticks closer than a brother and that a friend loves at all times. This means it's important for me to be a good friend always—not just when times are fun. I need to stick with my friends in hard times, through challenges and heartbreaking moments. Please help me be the kind of friend I would like to have, even when it's uncomfortable. Please help me be dependable and caring. Help me discover new ways to make my friends' days better. Please help me encourage and love my friends well, out of the abundant love You've given me. In Jesus' name I pray, amen.

Think about it!
How can you be a better friend?

CHOOSE YOUR WORDS

"Whoever would love life and see good days must keep their tongue from evil and their lips from deceitful speech."

1 PETER 3:10 NIV

Lord Jesus, I would love every day to be a good day. The thought of loving my life—instead of just enduring or even hating it—is really fantastic. I would like to enjoy and appreciate my life. I often forget that my mouth and my words have the power to change everything—including my outlook on life. Please help me learn that what I choose to say—or not say—makes a huge difference. Help me keep my tongue from evil and my lips from deceiving others. I don't want to be two-faced. I don't want to say things that hurt others or bring shame to You, Lord. Please help me to choose my words wisely so that I may have a good life! In Your name I pray, amen.

Think about it!

Why is it important to think before you speak?

FOCUS

Since, then, you have been raised with Christ,
set your hearts on things above, where Christ
is, seated at the right hand of God.
COLOSSIANS 3:1 NIV

Father, thank You for Your Son, Jesus! Thank You for His perfect life—and His complete sacrifice that paid for my sins. It's tempting to focus on myself and the things of this world, but I pray that You would help me seek things that are above. I don't want to think selfish, me-me-me thoughts all the time. Instead, set my mind and the direction of my life on You and the truth of Your Word. Help me live a life of love and faith in You. Help me to avoid getting bogged down with what other teenagers think is important—grades, clothes, electronics, relationships, popularity. . . Help me focus on You and You alone. In Jesus' name I pray, amen.

Think about it!
What are some "things above" that
should have your attention?

TRUSTWORTHY

Blessed is the man who makes the Lord his trust, who does not turn to the proud, to those who go astray after a lie!

PSALM 40:4 ESV

Father, I'm so glad You're trustworthy. I'm so thankful You are my God. And I'm grateful I can put my trust in You and You alone. I don't want to do life apart from You—not ever! This world is filled with so many people and things that are fighting for my attention and affection. I don't want my heart to follow a lie. I don't want to give my time and attention to anything that would lead me away from You. Please help me realize what is stealing my attention from You, Lord— and help me turn away from those things. I want to keep my eyes on You, always and forever. In Jesus' name I pray, amen.

Think about it!
Why is God trustworthy?

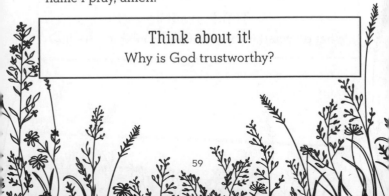

MY REASON FOR HOPE

Let us hold unswervingly to the hope we profess, for he who promised is faithful.
HEBREWS 10:23 NIV

Father God, I put my faith in You. I believe You are who You say You are. I believe Jesus is Your perfect Son, who came to pay for my sins with His life. I trust You, and I expect all You've promised will happen in Your perfect timing. Time and time again You've proven Yourself to be constant in my life. It's wonderful that I can always look forward to what You'll do next. I may not know what each day will bring, but I do know that You are faithful. Even if things look or feel messy right now, You can and will make something absolutely beautiful from my mess. Thank You! In Jesus' name I pray, amen.

Think about it!
What do you think God might do next in your life?

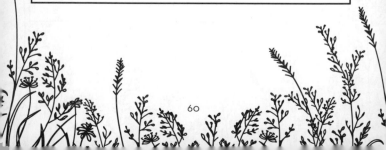

PUTTING OTHERS FIRST

*Do nothing out of selfish ambition or vain
conceit. Rather, in humility value others above
yourselves, not looking to your own interests
but each of you to the interests of the others.*
PHILIPPIANS 2:3–4 NIV

Father, pride has such a sneaky way of creeping into
my life. I think I'm better than I really am. I feel like
I deserve so much. But, really, I should want to live
like Jesus did—and He was totally humble. He gave up
everything to come to earth as a man. He didn't come
as a king, living in a luxurious palace with a bunch of
servants. No. Instead, He came to serve others. Please
help me to stop focusing on my own interests and
instead take notice of what other people need. Help
me figure out how to best help them without thinking
of what's in it for me. In Jesus' name I pray, amen.

Think about it!
How can putting the needs of others
first change your heart?

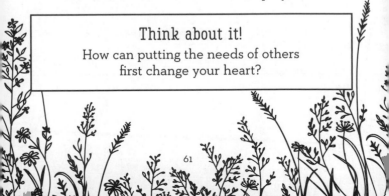

ANGER ISSUES

Be not quick in your spirit to become angry,
for anger lodges in the heart of fools.
ECCLESIASTES 7:9 ESV

Heavenly Father, sometimes I get super angry—or I feel anger brewing inside me. I know I shouldn't be this way. And really, I don't like getting angry because I know it affects every part of me. It feels like it gets lodged in my heart and changes the way I think and speak and respond to others—and to You. When I'm tempted to let anger build up and simmer, could You please extinguish it? Please help me remember that life is too short to waste my time getting angry. Instead, please help me find a better way to deal with my frustration, let it go, and move on. Thank You for filling me with Your Holy Spirit, who can help me get past my anger issues. In Jesus' name I pray, amen.

Think about it!
What is the best way to deal with anger?

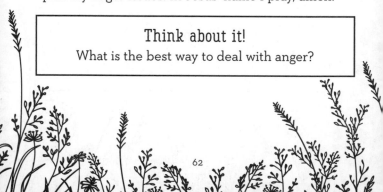

I LOVE YOU!

Though you have not seen him, you love him.
Though you do not now see him, you believe in
him and rejoice with joy that is inexpressible
and filled with glory, obtaining the outcome
of your faith, the salvation of your souls.
1 PETER 1:8–9 ESV

Jesus, faith is a pretty exciting thing. Even though I've never seen You, I believe in You. I know You're real. I know You're alive. And I love You. And, in my trust and faith, You fill me with joy that I can't explain. Sometimes it feels like I might explode with joy! Help me live out my faith in You, Lord. I want my joy and peace to be contagious. I want to love people really, really, really well. Thank You for saving me and filling me with this bubbling-up-inside kind of joy. In Your name I pray, amen.

Think about it!
What is faith?

BEAUTY. . .AND THE BEAST?

Like a gold ring in a pig's snout is a
beautiful woman without discretion.
PROVERBS 11:22 ESV

Father, I admit that I focus on my looks—sometimes too much. And I begin to wonder, for some reason, what I should change or how I could change my appearance. In my own way, I try to figure out how to make myself look more desirable—either to other people or myself. Father, I pray that I'll become content with the way You created me. I want my true beauty to be found in my heart. Please help me to focus not just on my looks but on wisdom and judgment too, so I don't end up like a gold ring in a pig's snout! I pray my life will be precious and valuable and not a foolish waste. In Jesus' name I pray, amen.

Think about it!
What makes a person truly beautiful?

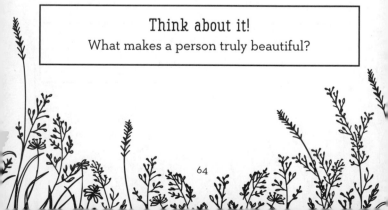

STEP BY STEP

My steps have held fast to Your paths.
My feet have not slipped.
PSALM 17:5 NASB

Father God, knowing that You'll direct each of my steps is a huge comfort. I pray that I'll willingly stick to Your paths, not wandering outside Your will. As You guide me, You won't let my feet slip. I don't have to worry about stumbling and falling when I'm walking through life with You. Even if I don't know where I'm going in the future, I'll confidently walk the path You have for me right now. I trust that You know where You're taking me, and You'll stay with me when the road gets rough. Thank You for lovingly guiding me and for having a good plan for my life. In Jesus' name I pray, amen.

Think about it!
How can you know with certainty that you're on the path God wants for you?

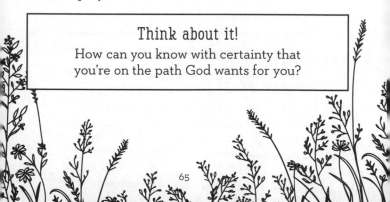

CHOOSING MY FRIENDS

*Blessed is the one who does not walk in step
with the wicked or stand in the way that sinners
take or sit in the company of mockers, but
whose delight is in the law of the LORD, and
who meditates on his law day and night.*

PSALM 1:1–2 NIV

Lord, I need wisdom when it comes to choosing my friends. I don't want to spend time with people whose bad habits could rub off on me. Your Word tells me that bad company corrupts good character, and that means I am affected and changed—for better or worse—by my friends. So, Father, I ask that You'd surround me with friends who love You as much as I do. Please help us to know Your Word better and challenge each other to live out Your truth in all we say and do. In Jesus' name I pray, amen.

Think about it!

Are there any friends in your life who are influencing you with their bad choices and habits? If yes, what should you do about it?

ASHAMED?

"If anyone is ashamed of me and my words in this adulterous and sinful generation, the Son of Man will be ashamed of them when he comes in his Father's glory with the holy angels."

MARK 8:38 NIV

Lord, I hate to admit this, but You know everything anyway—and I feel like I need to confess. Sometimes I'm afraid to stand up for You. When people say awful things or use Your name in vain, I stay silent. Could You please help me be bolder for You, Lord? I'm not ashamed of You and Your words. At least I don't want to be. Could You please help me stand up for Your truth—to stand up for You? I want to be a good example and witness for You in this world. I love You. In Jesus' name I pray, amen.

Think about it!
How can you be bold for Jesus?

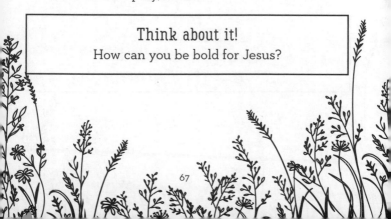

SETTING AN EXAMPLE

Don't let anyone look down on you because you are young, but set an example for the believers in speech, in conduct, in love, in faith and in purity.

1 TIMOTHY 4:12 NIV

Father God, in the grand scheme of things, I'm just a teensy blip in the picture of eternity. And still, I hope You'll use me to make a difference in the world. Please help me make my family better just by being a part of it. Help me step out in boldness and faith and make my school a better place. Even if it takes a lot of effort and a lot less selfishness, please help me make life better for people who meet me. In other words, please make my life count. Make my existence matter. And help me improve the lives of everyone who knows me. In Jesus' name I pray, amen.

Think about it!
What can you do to be a courageous world-changer?

GUARANTEED

In him you also, when you heard the word of truth, the gospel of your salvation, and believed in him, were sealed with the promised Holy Spirit, who is the guarantee of our inheritance until we acquire possession of it, to the praise of his glory.

Ephesians 1:13–14 esv

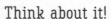

Lord, thank You for Your Holy Spirit. Thank You for the gift He is to believers like me. It might be awhile until I see You in heaven but until then, Your Spirit is proof that I'm Yours. I've been saved through faith in Jesus. And I've been sealed, or protected, through Your Holy Spirit. So I praise You, Lord! Thank You for Your plan and providing something I could never do on my own. Thank You for Jesus. And thank You for the way Your Spirit secures my future with You. In Jesus' name I pray, amen.

Think about it!
How does it feel to know your eternal future is secure with Jesus?

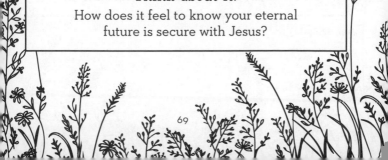

COME WITH CONFIDENCE

*Let us then approach God's throne of grace
with confidence, so that we may receive mercy
and find grace to help us in our time of need.*
HEBREWS 4:16 NIV

Father, so often I feel like I can only come to You if I have my act all together. And because I feel like a hot, imperfect mess, sometimes I feel like I shouldn't come to You at all. Yet You promise that I can approach You with confidence. You have a throne of grace—undeserved favor! And when I come near to You, You lavish me with mercy and grace. You rescue me when I need it most. I need Your forgiveness and comfort, Lord. I draw near to You tonight. Please bless me with joy and peace as I rest and hope in You. I love You. In Jesus' name I pray, amen.

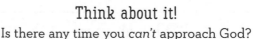

Think about it!
Is there any time you *can't* approach God?

WHY WORRY?

*"Therefore do not worry about tomorrow,
for tomorrow will worry about itself. Each
day has enough trouble of its own."*

MATTHEW 6:34 NIV

Father God, I believe in Your Word. I really do know it's true. But I desperately need assurance that it's true tonight. Lord, I'm nervous about tomorrow. I know Your Word tells me I don't have to worry about tomorrow. But I feel myself on the verge of obsessing and getting anxious about things. When I'm stressed, please replace those feelings with peace. When I'm dwelling on everything that *could* happen, help me stick to the facts and not get overwhelmed by the what-ifs. And when I start physically feeling the effects of my anxiety, please help me take a deep breath and relax. Thank You that I can trust in You completely. In Jesus' name I pray, amen.

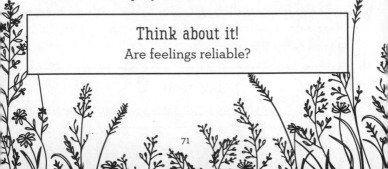

Think about it!
Are feelings reliable?

PREVENTING A CALLUS

He said, "Go and tell this people: 'Be ever
hearing, but never understanding; be ever
seeing, but never perceiving.' Make the heart
of this people calloused; make their ears dull
and close their eyes. Otherwise they might see
with their eyes, hear with their ears, understand
with their hearts, and turn and be healed."
ISAIAH 6:9–10 NIV

Father, I know You can make hearts calloused, just
like You can make ears dull or eyes closed. Please
help me understand that every time I turn from You
and Your commands, I get a callus. And eventually,
over time, they build up—and then I can't hear You or
see You at work. I want to hear *and* understand You. I
want to see *and* recognize You. Please keep my heart
tender to You and Your leading. Shape me into the
young woman You want me to become—a girl who's
quick to listen and obey. I want to see with my eyes,
hear with my ears, and understand with my heart. In
Jesus' name I pray, amen.

Think about it!
What is the best way to prevent a calloused heart?

NO, NOT ONE

"None is righteous, no, not one; no one understands; no one seeks for God. All have turned aside; together they have become worthless; no one does good, not even one."
ROMANS 3:10–12 ESV

Heavenly Father, why do people turn away from You? Why don't they chase after You? How I want to be different from everyone else! On my own, I'm imperfect. I try to avoid sin, but perfection and righteousness are things I could never accomplish on my own. Perfection is through Jesus alone, and it's to Him I turn. I don't want to turn aside. I don't want to become worthless. Through Jesus, I can do good here on earth. While I have breath in my lungs, please count me righteous through Christ alone. In Jesus' name I pray, amen.

Think about it!
What good can you do with the help of Jesus while you're here on earth?

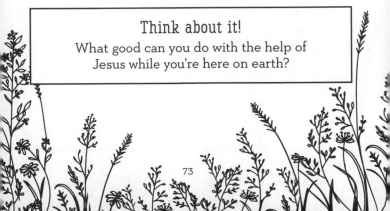

SCHOOL STRUGGLES

A sluggard's appetite is never filled, but the desires of the diligent are fully satisfied.
PROVERBS 13:4 NIV

Father, I'm glad I can come to You at any time about anything. Lately I've been super frustrated with a certain subject at school. As much as I want to succeed, something's just not clicking. I don't know what to change or how to improve. And so, I need Your help. Please help things make sense. Help me to muster up the strength and determination to work as hard as I can. I want to work for You—and You alone. Please curb my anxiety about the pressure to succeed. Even when this class is difficult and confusing, I trust You'll help me focus on working hard to glorify You. In Jesus' name I pray, amen.

Think about it!
What struggles are you facing at school?

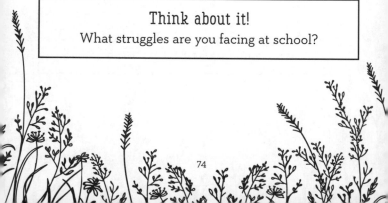

KEEP YOUR WAY PURE

How can a young person stay on the path of purity?
By living according to your word. I seek you with all
my heart; do not let me stray from your commands.

PSALM 119:9-10 NIV

Father, it's sometimes hard to know what's right—and
then follow through with it. Please help me to seek
out truth in Your Word then live by it. Please keep
my feet on the path of purity. I seek You with all my
heart, and I want to follow Your commands. Thank
You for guiding me to make good choices and live the
right way. There is a right way and a wrong way to live;
and there is a path of purity and a path of impurity.
Please help me stay on the right, pure path. I want to
be a good example of what it means to be a Christ
follower. In Jesus' name I pray, amen.

Think about it!
When you're confused about the right
way and the wrong way, where should
you go for guidance and truth?

PAYBACK?

*Make sure that nobody pays back wrong for
wrong, but always strive to do what is good
for each other and for everyone else.*

1 Thessalonians 5:15 niv

Lord Jesus, living for You can be difficult. Sometimes I
feel selfish and want to do what feels right for me. And
when people treat me poorly, so often my first thought
is figuring out a way I can get revenge. But I'm Your
child—and You live in me. And so, I don't have to pay
back any wrong done to me. Instead, I can choose to
forgive others and treat them with kindness. Help me
to always do what is best for other people. Help me to
unselfishly look past my own agenda and interests—
past myself and to the needs of others. I want to be
a good example for You. In Your name I pray, amen.

Think about it!
How does it feel to look past your own
interests and consider others instead?

NO REGRETS

For the sorrow that is according to the will of God produces a repentance without regret, leading to salvation, but the sorrow of the world produces death.

2 CORINTHIANS 7:10 NASB

Father God, so many people live with regrets. And often, the choices I make seem wrong. Sometimes I can't believe the things I say or do. Can You help me? I want to make choices that honor You—choices that will help me live a life with zero regrets. In the heat of the moment, please give me enough wisdom to choose what pleases You. I pray that I'll be able to live tomorrow without regrets. But if, or when, I do make a bad choice, please help me to quickly realize it and repent—not continue in my sin and add to my trouble. Please guide me. I want to follow You always! In Jesus' name I pray, amen.

Think about it!
What steps can you take to ensure you live a zero-regrets life?

CHOSEN

Therefore, as God's chosen people, holy and dearly loved, clothe yourselves with compassion, kindness, humility, gentleness and patience.
COLOSSIANS 3:12 NIV

Father, You chose me! Every time I'm tempted to listen to voices that tell me I'm unwanted or not good enough, please remind me that You, the holy God of the universe, chose me. Help me to truly know it, and then help me to live like it! Help me to notice the people who need compassion—and then please give me the strength and courage I need to reach out in love and understanding. If I'm being honest, there are plenty of people in this world I'd rather not be kind to, but I know that kindness is possible through Your Holy Spirit. Please guard my life against pride and thinking too highly of myself. Instead, please help me treat others as You'd treat them, Lord. In Jesus' name I pray, amen.

Think about it!
How does it feel to know that God chose *you*?

TRUST AND OBEY

Therefore, my dear friends, as you have always obeyed—not only in my presence, but now much more in my absence—continue to work out your salvation with fear and trembling, for it is God who works in you to will and to act in order to fulfill his good purpose.

PHILIPPIANS 2:12–13 NIV

Father God, I want to obey You today and every day. When I feel like doing my own thing and living life my way, please help me to remember that You'll direct my paths. What a comfort and a gift! I honor and respect You, Lord. And I trust that You'll keep working in my life. Please fulfill Your wonderful purpose for me. I'm humbled that You have a good purpose for me, and I fully trust that You'll act to make it happen. Thanks for choosing to use me. In Jesus' name I pray, amen.

Think about it!
How is God using you to help grow His kingdom?

NOTHING

*For I am convinced that neither death nor
life, neither angels nor demons, neither the
present nor the future, nor any powers, neither
height nor depth, nor anything else in all
creation, will be able to separate us from the
love of God that is in Christ Jesus our Lord.*
ROMANS 8:38–39 NIV

Lord Jesus, the fact that absolutely nothing can or will
separate me from God's love is so amazing. *Nothing*
will separate me from the love found in You. Nothing
in this life—not even death. Nothing I did in my past or
am doing right now. Nothing I'll do in the future. Not
angels or demons or anything else that's been or ever
will be created. I'm completely safe and secure in Your
love. This alone will help me sleep sweetly, resting in
You tonight. I love You. In Jesus' name I pray, amen.

Think about it!
Is there *anything* that can separate
you from God's love?

WHO'S IN CONTROL?

*Trust in him at all times, O people; pour out
your heart before him; God is a refuge for us.*
PSALM 62:8 ESV

Father, tonight I need assurance that You're in charge.
Right now, I feel like everything has spun out of my
control. Control is such an illusion, isn't it? Please
help me rest in the fact that You know so much more
than I do about what is going on—and You know what
I really need and what is best for me. Deep down, I'm
afraid to let go of my hopes and dreams and place
them in Your hands. But I know that I need to do it,
and I want to release them to You. Please fill me with
Your peace as I trust You with my life. In Jesus' name
I pray, amen.

Think about it!
What do you think will happen when
you put everything in God's hands?

DOING A U-TURN

"Repent! Turn away from all your offenses;
then sin will not be your downfall."

ᴇᴢᴇᴋɪᴇʟ 18:30 ɴɪᴠ

Father, I have sinned against You. Today I gave in to temptation, and I'm feeling so ashamed and unworthy. Please forgive me. I want to repent—not just ask for forgiveness, but truly change and turn from my sin. Like a car doing a U-turn, I want to go in the opposite direction—and toward right choices that honor You. When Satan reminds me of my past mistakes, please help me remember Your forgiveness. Jesus died for me; He was a perfect sacrifice for all my sins, including those today. I don't deserve what Jesus did for me, but I'm so very thankful. Thank You, Lord, for forgiveness that I don't deserve and favor I never could earn. In Jesus' name I pray, amen.

Think about it!
How much does God love you?

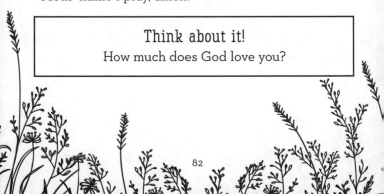

PREPARED FOR ACTION

*Therefore, prepare your minds for action, keep sober
in spirit, fix your hope completely on the grace to
be brought to you at the revelation of Jesus Christ.*
1 PETER 1:13 NASB

Lord, this world is a difficult place. You know that—
and it's why You came to save me. As I drift off to
sleep, please prepare my mind for action. Help me
understand that I can't just drift through life—I need
to be serious about it. I need to protect my heart. I
need to focus my mind. I want and need to fix all my
hope on You and Your grace. When I'm tempted to
go my own way, please reel me back in. Instead of
floating along and encountering whatever comes my
way, please remind me that I need to actively live in
Your truth and make decisions that point to You and
Your goodness in my life. In Your name I pray, amen.

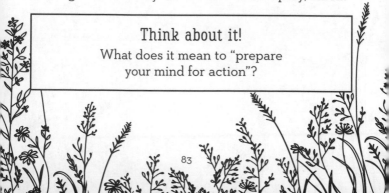

Think about it!
What does it mean to "prepare
your mind for action"?

RESTORE WHAT'S BROKEN

When the LORD takes pleasure in anyone's way, he causes their enemies to make peace with them.

PROVERBS 16:7 NIV

Father God, thank You for Your gift of peace. Thank You for Your peace that ushers in completeness and calm. I'm both amazed and grateful that You have the power to restore what's broken and out of sorts—even relationships. Sometimes it feels like it's impossible for me to make peace with someone when our relationship has been broken—or maybe the relationship never felt whole in the first place. But You, Father. . . You make things right. You even cause my enemies to make peace with me. Please continue to mend what's broken in my life, especially when it comes to how I relate to others. May the things I say and do honor and please You. In Jesus' name I pray, amen.

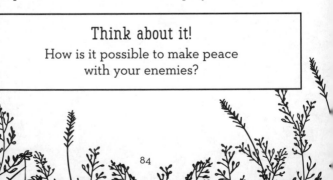

Think about it!
How is it possible to make peace with your enemies?

WORDS AND MEDITATIONS

*Let the words of my mouth and the meditation
of my heart be acceptable in your sight,
O LORD, my rock and my redeemer.*
PSALM 19:14 ESV

Father, lately I've been obsessing over something—and I can't stop thinking about it. I've been obsessing so much that it could be considered an idol at this point. Would You please help me readjust my thinking? I want to keep my eyes and focus on You. I want what my heart dwells on to be acceptable in Your sight, Lord—and that means not being consumed by the thoughts and concerns and desires of the world. As difficult as it may be to readjust my thinking, I want to do it. Please help me. Please transform me by renewing my mind. In Jesus' name I pray, amen.

Think about it!
What is your heart and mind focusing on tonight?

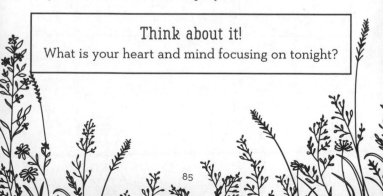

GOD IS *FOR* YOU!

What, then, shall we say in response to these things? If God is for us, who can be against us?

ROMANS 8:31 NIV

Father God, it is so good to be known and loved by You. It feels so wonderful to know that You are *for* me. And when You are for me, Lord, no one else can be against me. Sure, it doesn't seem like everyone always likes me; but when it comes down to it, You're in control of all. You can and do change people's hearts. And You can and do change situations. I pray that I'll boldly trust You and live out my faith, fully confident that I can follow Your leading. Thank You for the amazing way You care for me! In Jesus' name I pray, amen.

Think about it!
What does "God is *for* you" truly mean?

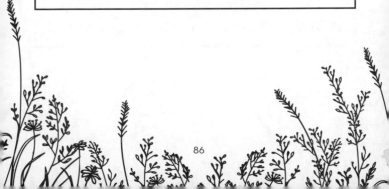

CREATED ON PURPOSE

*I will give thanks to You, for I am fearfully
and wonderfully made; wonderful are Your
works, and my soul knows it very well.*

PSALM 139:14 NASB

Lord, Your Word says that I am fearfully and wonderfully made. It means so much that You say that, but sometimes I don't really believe it. Deep down, I have doubts. I don't always like the way I look. Some days I don't like my hair. Other days it's my face. And I wish my body were different. Yet You made me just the way I am. As the master artist, You believe I am beautiful. You created me to look like this because it was Your plan. When I'm unhappy with the way I look, remind me that You see me. You know me. And You love me—just as I am. Thank You for making me in an amazing and unique way. In Jesus' name I pray, amen.

Think about it!

Look in the mirror and remind yourself that God created every single part of you on purpose, just as it is. How does that make you feel?

ALIVE!

But God, being rich in mercy, because of the great love with which he loved us, even when we were dead in our trespasses, made us alive together with Christ—by grace you have been saved.

EPHESIANS 2:4–5 ESV

Father, You are so generous with Your mercy—mercy I don't deserve, and mercy I can't earn. Thank You for Your forgiveness and Your grace—these gifts bring me to life in Christ. Thank You for saving me. Thank You for loving me so very much, even when I was far from You. Tonight, as I think about all that's happened today, I'm thankful that I can take some time to think about what really, truly matters: You and Your mercy and love and saving grace. Even when life's little details try to crowd out what's important, I will take moments in my day to fully appreciate You and Your wonderful gifts. In Jesus' name I pray, amen.

Think about it!
Why does God give us all the good things we *don't* deserve?

BUILDING UP

Therefore encourage one another
and build each other up.
1 THESSALONIANS 5:11 NIV

Lord, sometimes I say and do things I regret later. Every once in a while, I'm moody, and I don't like what I think or say when I'm in a bad mood. But I don't know how to change. I *do* know I want to be a bright spot in the lives of others. And I want to be a good example for You. When I'm tempted to tear other people down in my grumpiness, please stop my words. When I'm on the verge of disrespecting my parents because they don't understand what I'm going through, please help me honor them with the words I say and my body language too. When I'd love to use a snappy but hurtful comeback, please shut the door to my mouth. Transform my moods, words, thoughts, and actions so they please You. In Jesus' name I pray, amen.

Think about it!
What are some words you could say to build up a friend or family member?

DO YOU BELIEVE THIS?

Jesus said to her, "I am the resurrection and the life. Whoever believes in me, though he die, yet shall he live, and everyone who lives and believes in me shall never die. Do you believe this?"

JOHN 11:25–26 ESV

Jesus, I believe You are the resurrection and the life! Thank You for coming to earth so people like me can believe in You and have life that lasts forever. I'm thankful that all I need to do is believe. It's amazing, really! I don't need to earn my way to an eternity with You. Belief in You can be so simple, but sometimes it's quite hard to do. But tonight, Lord, I want to affirm that I believe in You. Thank You for the forever life You've promised. You are so, so good to me! I love You. In Your name I pray, amen.

Think about it!
What are all the reasons you believe in Jesus?

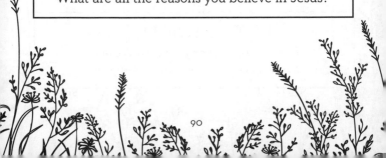

SWEET SLEEP

In vain you rise early and stay up late, toiling for
food to eat—for he grants sleep to those he loves.
PSALM 127:2 NIV

Lord God, I'm having such a hard time falling asleep tonight. When I toss and turn, it feels like I can't turn my brain off. I can't seem to stop thinking about what happened yesterday, the events of today. . .or what could be coming tomorrow. Would You please quiet my mind—hit the OFF switch to my thoughts? I ask for Your peace, Father—the peace that only comes from You. And in that peace, I pray I can find rest. Please help me sleep peacefully tonight so I can wake up refreshed tomorrow morning, ready to serve and worship You. In Jesus' name I pray, amen.

Think about it!
What helps you relax and fall asleep each night?

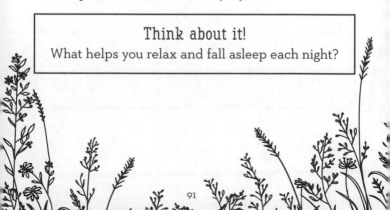

ARE YOU WITH ME?

*The LORD was with Joseph and gave
him success in whatever he did.*
GENESIS 39:23 NIV

Father, Your Word is filled with so many stories about men and women who lived thousands of years ago. Even if the stories seem like ancient history to me, I can still learn valuable lessons from their lives and the ways You worked in and through them. I can learn so much from a man like Joseph, who fully trusted You. It's so encouraging that You were with him, no matter what. Even when he had every reason to despair about his future—even when he was locked up in prison—You were with him, preparing him for success. Lord, be with me as You were with Joseph. Please bless what I say and do. Give me success. In Jesus' name I pray, amen.

Think about it!
Is the Lord with you on your good days? What about bad days too? How do you know for sure?

COME NEAR

Come near to God and he will come near to you.
JAMES 4:8 NIV

Father God, I'm sorry for wandering away from You so easily. I get distracted by the things of this world and the busyness of life. And while it isn't an excuse, it's just what I do sometimes. Please forgive me. I want to be near You. Father, tonight I want to feel You drawing me toward You. I pray You'll fill my heart with Your peace and love. I love You and want to be able to shut out all the noise of the world and focus on You and You alone. You've given me all of Yourself through Your Son. How much of *me* do *You* have, though? Help me to not be afraid to give You all of me—all that I have, and all that I am. In Jesus' name I pray, amen.

Think about it!
Have you given Jesus all of you? Why or why not?

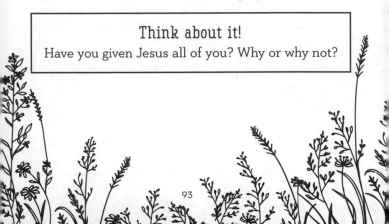

TAMING MY TONGUE

*The one who has knowledge uses
words with restraint, and whoever has
understanding is even-tempered.*
PROVERBS 17:27 NIV

Lord Jesus, sometimes I wonder if what I say even matters. Are words really *that* important? But then I remember You are the Word made flesh. You matter. And what You say matters. Similarly, what I say really does matter. Please help me pay close attention to the words I speak. When I'm tempted to blurt out every single thought that comes to mind, help me understand the importance of controlling my tongue. Please help me remember that I can and should honor You with my words. Please help me speak with restraint (even though it's so hard!). In Your name I pray, amen.

Think about it!
How can you honor Jesus with your words?

WHERE ARE YOU?

My God, I cry out by day, but you do not answer, by night, but I find no rest.

PSALM 22:2 NIV

Father, sometimes when I pray, it feels like my prayers are just bouncing back to me—like You don't hear them. Deep down, though, I know You hear. I know You care. But it can be so discouraging when I have to wait for an answer from You. Help me continue to trust even when it feels like You're not there. Help me be a patient waiter. Would You please give me peace during the wait? I want to be close to You, Lord, and so I will keep praying in faith. Morning and night and all throughout the day, I will share my feelings with You. Please help my faith grow as I wait for You. In Jesus' name I pray, amen.

Think about it!
Does God want to hear *all* your thoughts and feelings?

LET MY LIGHT SHINE

*"You are the light of the world. A city set
on a hill cannot be hidden. . . . In the same
way, let your light shine before others, so
that they may see your good works and give
glory to your Father who is in heaven."*
MATTHEW 5:14, 16 ESV

Lord, I'm so glad You came to earth, not only to save
those who would believe in You, but also to teach truth.
Honestly, it's a little overwhelming to know that I'm
light in this world. Light always drives away darkness,
so I ask that You'd use me as a light wherever I go.
Please give me courage to stand up for what I believe
in—for what is true. Please help me keep in mind that
where I am right now is temporary, but my soul is
eternal. Help me live each day with this in mind. In
Your name I pray, amen.

Think about it!
In what ways did you "shine your light" today?

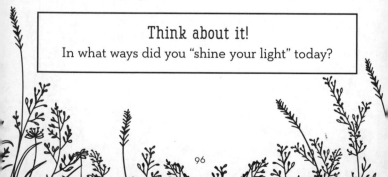

WORTH SO MUCH MORE

"Are not two sparrows sold for a penny? Yet not one of them will fall to the ground outside your Father's care. And even the very hairs of your head are all numbered. So don't be afraid; you are worth more than many sparrows."

MATTHEW 10:29–31 NIV

God, You are Alpha and Omega, the Beginning and the End. You are the creator and sustainer of all life. The fact that You are all-knowing is awesome and amazing; it's also a little scary! But I come to You humbled, Lord, with a well-deserved respect and honor of You. I'm not worthy of Your mercy, but You've lavished me with it anyway. I'm in awe of how generous You are and how Your love and forgiveness are such undeserved gifts of favor. Thank You. You are a good, good God! In Jesus' name I pray, amen.

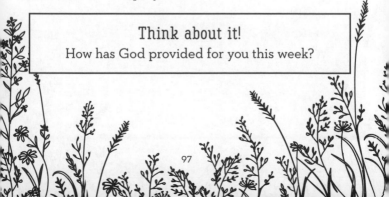

Think about it!
How has God provided for you this week?

WHATEVER YOU DO

*And whatever you do, whether in word or deed,
do it all in the name of the Lord Jesus, giving
thanks to God the Father through him.*

COLOSSIANS 3:17 NIV

Father God, I want to honor You in everything I do and say—and I want people to be able to see Jesus living in me. I admit this isn't always easy. Sometimes I struggle to remember to watch what I say. If You need to, Lord, please keep a door over my mouth. . . and don't hesitate to shut it. If that's what it takes to keep me from saying things that don't glorify You, then I'm willing. I thank You, Father, for the voice You've given me. Please help me use it to share Your love and kindness with the world. And thank You for the ability to do things for You. Please use me to reach this world for You! In Jesus' name I pray, amen.

Think about it!

Why is it important to use your voice for God?

SHINE LIKE STARS

Do everything without grumbling or arguing, so that you may become blameless and pure, "children of God without fault in a warped and crooked generation." Then you will shine among them like stars in the sky as you hold firmly to the word of life.
PHILIPPIANS 2:14–16 NIV

Father God, tonight I confess that it's really easy to spend a lot of time grumbling and complaining. But every time I do, I end up being hypercritical. I waste so much time looking for what's wrong or annoying that I miss everything good. I want to be without fault in this "crooked generation." I want to live like Your child and shine like a star in the sky. So, Lord, I need to give up my tendency to grumble. I need to hold on to Your Word of life and let it shine through what I say, do, and think about. In Jesus' name I pray, amen.

Think about it!
Do you spend a lot of time complaining and looking for the negative? If so, how can you turn it around so you're not missing out on all the good right in front of you?

A NEW THING

"Forget the former things; do not dwell on the past. See, I am doing a new thing! Now it springs up; do you not perceive it?"

ISAIAH 43:18–19 NIV

Father, I praise You for being God Almighty, full of power. I know I should be content with where You have me in life—because You have a good purpose and plan for me. But sometimes I wish I could have a fresh start. I feel stuck; but I trust that someday You'll bring changes into my life. Please help me get unstuck. Help me make wise choices that glorify You. And when You do bring something new into my life, please help me remember where I've come from. While I don't want to dwell on the past, I also don't want to forget how far You've brought me and how You've worked in my life. I love You, Lord! In Jesus' name I pray, amen.

Think about it!
What new things have God brought into your life?

YOU ARE MY TRUST

*For you, O Lord, are my hope, my
trust, O LORD, from my youth.*
PSALM 71:5 ESV

Lord, sometimes I have trust issues. I don't trust many
people. And at times, I even find myself wondering if
You're truly trustworthy. But really, I need to ask myself:
How could I *not* trust You? You're completely worthy of
my trust. I mean, you keep every one of You promises!
You're *the only one* who keeps all the promises You've
made. What would my life be like without You, Lord?
I'm so thankful to know You. My life would be empty
and sad without Your guidance! Who, or what, could
I trust in if it wasn't for You? Thank You for keeping
Your promises and being 100 percent trustworthy. In
Jesus' name I pray, amen.

Think about it!
Why should you trust God with everything?

MY POWERFUL GOD

"He did this so that all the peoples of the earth might know that the hand of the LORD is powerful and so that you might always fear the LORD your God."
JOSHUA 4:24 NIV

Father God, all throughout history, You've made a way for Your people. You protect and provide for Your children. Your hand has worked powerfully in the lives of those who believe in You—including mine. I know the great things You have done for me—things I never could have done for myself. You treat me with so much kindness and favor. Thank You! I pray I'll always recognize the ways You've so faithfully and lovingly provided for me. You are all-powerful. You always have been, and You always will be. With You as my Lord and my God, who is there on earth to fear? No one! I praise You, Lord. In Jesus' name I pray, amen.

Think about it!
How has the Lord shown you His favor?

FOLLOWING YOUR LEAD

*By faith Abraham obeyed when he was
called to go out to a place that he was to
receive as an inheritance. And he went
out, not knowing where he was going.*

HEBREWS 11:8 ESV

Father, when I look at the life of Abraham in Genesis, You asked him to do a huge thing—to trust You with the unknown. You asked him to leave his home and follow You. Instead of choosing the comfortable and familiar, he chose to step out in faith and obey You. He had no idea where You would lead him; he only knew You *would* lead him. Just like Abraham, I pray that I'll be ready and willing to follow wherever You lead me. As I look to my future, I pray I'll have the courage to boldly do all that You ask me. Please make my way abundantly clear. In Jesus' name I pray, amen.

Think about it!
Do you fully trust God with the
unknown in your life?

WISHING AND HOPING

Many are the plans in a person's heart, but it is the LORD's purpose that prevails.
PROVERBS 19:21 NIV

Father God, You know that I have so many dreams for my future; and some plans I've made will hopefully make my wishes a reality. I know what I'd like to have happen in my life. But ultimately, Your purpose will prevail. You have plans for me. . .things I need to experience and issues I must face. I want to trust You, Lord—I *do* trust You. Please help me welcome Your will for me. If I need to change my hopes and dreams and plans to go along with Your purpose for my life, please help me be open to it. I'm so excited to see what You're going to do in my life and through me! In Jesus' name I pray, amen.

Think about it!
What are your hopes and dreams for the future?

LEAD ME

*The LORD is my shepherd, I lack nothing. He makes
me lie down in green pastures, he leads me beside
quiet waters, he refreshes my soul. He guides
me along the right paths for his name's sake.*

PSALM 23:1–3 NIV

Father, You've promised that Jesus will return—but
sometimes I'm afraid I won't know when He does. How
can I know? Your Word says that many people will
come and falsely claim they're Jesus. But Your Word
also promises that Your sheep—Your children—will
know their Shepherd's voice. Please help my heart
know Your voice. I love Jesus. He is my Shepherd. I
trust He will lead me and that I'll faithfully listen to
Him and obey. I'm so thankful He provides all I need.
Please help me rest in the fact that I am Yours, and
You'll never lead me astray. In Jesus' name I pray, amen.

Think about it!
How will you know the voice of the Shepherd?

WISE FRIENDS

Whoever walks with the wise becomes wise,
but the companion of fools will suffer harm.
PROVERBS 13:20 ESV

Lord, I sometimes overlook the importance of choosing my friends wisely. It's tempting to try to fit in with the popular crowd—or at least a bunch of friends who want to spend time with me. But instead of focusing so much on what's on the outside, please help me to see what my "friends" are really like. Are they leading me away from You? Are they influencing me to do things that are sinful or not very healthy for me? I pray I would make right, holy choices. If my friends can't help me do that, please bring other friends into my life. I'd love to become wise. Please keep me from making foolish friend choices. In Jesus' name I pray, amen.

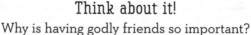

Think about it!
Why is having godly friends so important?

WALKING IN THE LIGHT

But if we walk in the light, as he is in the light,
we have fellowship with one another, and the
blood of Jesus his Son cleanses us from all sin.
1 JOHN 1:7 ESV

Father, I know what it's like to be afraid of the dark. When I was younger, nighttime was sometimes spooky; night lights and flashlights were helpful because the light drove away the darkness. Just like the dark of night is less scary when there's light, it's much easier to walk through my life with Your light. I am so thankful Jesus is the light of the world. I'm thankful to know Him. I'm thankful for the way Your Word is a lamp to my feet and a light for my path. And I'm thankful I don't have to stumble through the darkness of the world on my own—because You always light the way. I want to keep walking in Your light. In Jesus' name I pray, amen.

Think about it!
When darkness closes in, who—
or what—brings the light?

THE MOMENT

"Very truly I tell you, whoever hears my word and believes him who sent me has eternal life and will not be judged but has crossed over from death to life."

JOHN 5:24 NIV

Father, for You, belief is the dividing line between eternal life and eternal death. But I haven't always believed in You. In fact, there was a time in my life when I didn't. So, my very big, important questions tonight are "*Have* I believed in You?" and "When was the moment I chose to believe in Christ and trust that my eternal heavenly home was secure?" If I've never said it before, God, I *do* believe in You! I believe You sent Jesus to earth to die for my sins. And I trust my eternity with Him. I want to spend forever in heaven with You. It's in Jesus' name I pray, amen.

Think about it!

What words come to mind when you think of spending forever in heaven?

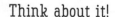

CREATED FOR GOOD WORKS

For we are His workmanship, created in Christ Jesus for good works, which God prepared beforehand so that we would walk in them.
EPHESIANS 2:10 NASB

Father, I'm blown away that You created me for good works—and that You've already prepared them for me! I really wish I could skip ahead and see what the future holds for me, but I'll try to be patient as I wait for You to reveal Your plan and purposes in Your perfect timing. It's hard for me to fathom how much You care for me and that You have a plan for my life. Please help me have courage and faith to follow Your leading and do all the good works You have called me to do. Please use me in amazing ways. I want to do Your will, Lord. In Jesus' name I pray, amen.

Think about it!
What are some amazing ways God might use you?

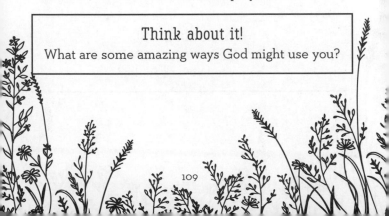

LIVING BY HIS WORD

*Be diligent to present yourself approved to
God as a workman who does not need to be
ashamed, accurately handling the word of truth.*
2 TIMOTHY 2:15 NASB

Thank You for Your Word, Lord. Thank You for its truth. Thank You that I can base my life on it. I want to understand the Bible more, Lord. I want to know more about it and memorize scriptures that can help me and guide me. Help me set aside a specific time to study Your Word. I pray it will transform my heart, my mind. . .my entire life. As it works in my heart, I trust it will show in my life. More than anything, Lord, I want You to approve of my thoughts, words, and actions. Please help me live a life pleasing to You. In Your name I pray, amen.

Think about it!
How can knowing the Bible better
help you live a good life?

A TRUSTWORTHY TEEN

A gossip betrays a confidence, but a trustworthy person keeps a secret.

PROVERBS 11:13 NIV

Father God, You created all things, including my mouth and my tongue. I can use my mouth and tongue to tell others about You and bring healing and life. Or I can use my words to hurt and destroy. When I choose to open my mouth and talk about other people, it's often hurtful. So, Lord, please help me to keep my mouth shut when I should. I want to become a trustworthy girl—worthy of the trust of others—and keep secrets when asked. I pray that I'll grow into a respectable, responsible young woman who knows when to speak and when to keep silent. I want to build people up with my words. Please help me think before I speak. In Jesus' name I pray, amen.

Think about it!
How can our words bring healing and life?

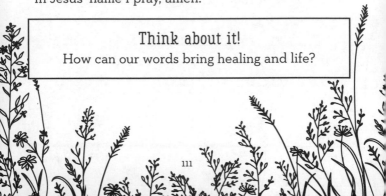

THE APPLE OF YOUR EYE

Keep me as the apple of your eye; hide
me in the shadow of your wings from the
wicked who are out to destroy me, from
my mortal enemies who surround me.
PSALM 17:8–9 NIV

Father God, You are my protector. You keep me safe.
When I imagine how a mama bird cares for her young
and would do anything to protect her babies, I know
the same is true for You when it comes to my well-
being and safety. You're always alert, always protecting, always watching out for my best. Thank You that
I don't have to live in fear of what people will try to
do to me. Thank You that even though enemies try to
destroy me—sometimes quite literally—You're the one
who protects me. I pray You'll continue to keep me
as the apple of Your eye. In Jesus' name I pray, amen.

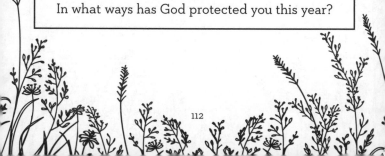

Think about it!
In what ways has God protected you this year?

SOMETHING SPECIAL

But you are a chosen people, a royal priesthood,
a holy nation, God's special possession, that
you may declare the praises of him who called
you out of darkness into his wonderful light.
1 PETER 2:9 NIV

Father, You have chosen me—it's almost too much to comprehend! I don't understand why You chose me, but I'm so thankful You did. Please help me remember that because of Jesus' sacrifice, I am royal and holy. Remind me that I am a princess—the daughter of the King of kings. As a much-loved possession of the Most High God, I pray that I'll boldly proclaim Your excellent wonders. Thank You for calling me out of the darkness and into Your marvelous light. Help me be a light to my friends and family who still are living in darkness. In Jesus' name I pray, amen.

Think about it!
Do you have the courage to make
a bold stand for Jesus?

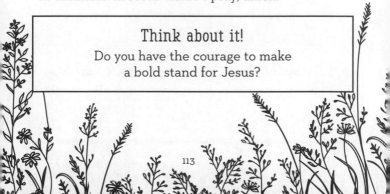

WITHOUT SIN

*Who can say, "I have kept my heart
pure; I am clean and without sin"?*
PROVERBS 20:9 NIV

Father, when I look around, I see so much wrong in
the world. So much sin. And people are celebrating
their sin. It's wrong. It's sad. And I know it grieves Your
heart to see it too. You sent Jesus into this world to
save every single human being, if they'd only recognize
Him as Lord. Thank You for sending Your Son. Thank
You for opening my eyes and heart to accept Him and
the sacrifice He made for me. Please forgive my sins.
And keep me humble, Father. Please remind me that
I'm no different—no better—than anyone else. We're all
sinners who need Jesus. Please help me reach people
You bring into my life with the good news of Jesus. In
His name I pray, amen.

Think about it!
Think about everyone you know. Who
needs to hear the good news of Jesus?

CHOOSE KINDNESS

If you really keep the royal law found in Scripture,
"Love your neighbor as yourself," you are doing
right. But if you show favoritism, you sin and
are convicted by the law as lawbreakers.

JAMES 2:8–9 NIV

Father, You created all people. But why are some people so awful? Since the garden of Eden, people have turned away from You to go their own ways. In the days of Noah, the wickedness of men grieved Your heart—and it still does. It breaks my heart when people say or do hurtful things too. Girls who purposefully exclude me crush my spirit, Father. Please help me look past the mean things people have said or done to me. Please help me to not look to them or their approval for my worth. Please help me remember that my value is in You. In Jesus' name I pray, amen.

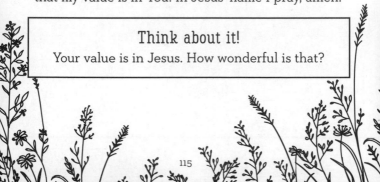

Think about it!
Your value is in Jesus. How wonderful is that?

CLEAN HANDS AND A PURE HEART

The one who has clean hands and a pure heart,
who does not trust in an idol or swear by a false
god. They will receive blessing from the LORD.

PSALM 24:4-5 NIV

Father, I confess that, at times, I'm tempted to cheat. To me, it often seems like no big deal, like looking off someone's paper at school or sneaking a peek at information I'm not meant to see or making sure things work out in my favor. In Your eyes, though, it's all cheating—and it's all wrong. Cheating is sinful—it misses the mark of what You've called me to as Your daughter. Lord, I confess my guilt. I pray You'll forgive me. Help me to repent and turn away from these habits. I want my conscience to be clean. I want to do what's right in Your eyes. In Jesus' name I pray, amen.

Think about it!
Why is cheating a sin?

TALK ABOUT IT

But in your hearts honor Christ the Lord as holy,
always being prepared to make a defense to
anyone who asks you for a reason for the hope that
is in you; yet do it with gentleness and respect.
1 PETER 3:15 ESV

Lord, I want to honor You and to always remember that, as much as You're my forever friend, You're also holy. When people ask me why I have hope or make choices different from other teenagers, please help me to gently share about You. I don't want to scare people away from You, but I also don't want to be so shy that my love for You stays hidden. I pray I'll be able to share Your truth while also respecting whomever I'm talking with. I want it to be natural for me to talk about You and how wonderful You are, Father. In Jesus' name I pray, amen.

Think about it!
What is the reason for your hope?

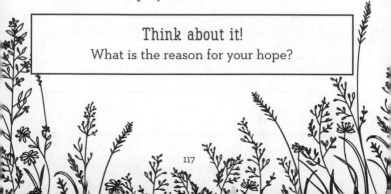

MERCY!

But when the kindness of God our Savior and His love for mankind appeared, He saved us, not on the basis of deeds which we have done in righteousness, but according to His mercy.

TITUS 3:4–5 NASB

Lord God, You are so kind! When people wonder where You are when bad things happen, I still see Your kindness and goodness all around me. You love us so much that You made a way for every single human being to be right with You. Through Your mercy, You saved us! There's no deed I must do to earn salvation and forever life in heaven with You. All I need to do is believe and welcome Your mercy. Tonight, I do—I *believe.* I believe in You. Thank You for saving me with Your generous mercy and grace. In Jesus' name I pray, amen.

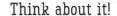

Think about it!

How would you respond to someone who asks why God lets bad things happen?

HOLY AND BLAMELESS

*He chose us in Him before the foundation
of the world, that we would be holy
and blameless before Him.*

Ephesians 1:4 NASB

Father God, I'm amazed that You would choose me before You even created the world. *Me! I'm chosen!* This concept seems strange to me—and yet, I'm forever grateful. Thank You for adopting me and bringing me into Your family. Thank You for Your undeserved favor so that I would and could be holy and blameless before You, the one and only holy and blameless God. You are loving and kind. I can do nothing that would make me deserving of Your precious grace. And so, Father, I come to You tonight to say thank You. I love You! In Jesus' name I pray, amen.

Think about it!
How big is God's family? How does
it feel to be a part of it?

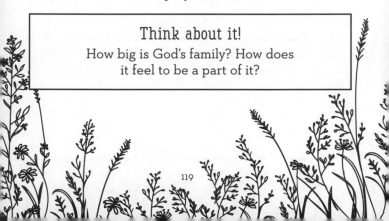

A NEW CREATION

*Therefore if anyone is in Christ, he is
a new creature; the old things passed
away; behold, new things have come.*

2 CORINTHIANS 5:17 NASB

Father God, thank You for the gift of new beginnings.
I love knowing that when I believed and trusted in
Your Son, I became a *new* creation. Everything in my
past—all the old things that alienated me and kept me
far from You—it's all dead and gone. You've replaced
all of it with new, wonderful, beautiful things! Thank
You for taking all that's old and wiping it away. Thank
You for making all things new. I pray that I'll fall asleep
tonight resting in this beautiful truth. I am a new creation in Christ! In His name I pray, amen.

Think about it!
How does God make us new when we believe and
ask Him to become Lord and leader of our lives?

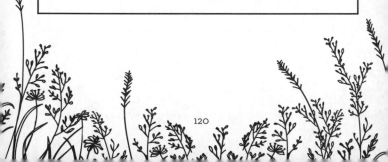

PEACE THAT I CAN'T UNDERSTAND

*And the peace of God, which surpasses
all understanding, will guard your hearts
and your minds in Christ Jesus.*

PHILIPPIANS 4:7 ESV

Father, I'm so glad that I can always be honest with You—I don't ever need to hide what I'm thinking or feeling. I feel so stressed out right now. I'm under overwhelming pressure. And I just want to do my best. Please help me remember that, no matter what, I can rest in You. Jesus promised that His yoke is easy and His burden is light. My burden is difficult and heavy right now. Help me give it to You. And, as I give You my burdens, Father, I pray You'll fill me with a deep peace that I can't explain or understand. Your peace would be so wonderful right now! Thank You! In Jesus' name I pray, amen.

Think about it!
Do you discuss *everything* with
Jesus? Why or why not?

IT'S A GOOD DAY!

When times are good, be happy; but when times are bad, consider this: God has made the one as well as the other.

ECCLESIASTES 7:14 NIV

Father God, I have good days and bad days—and today, I'm thankful for all the very good things You've done and are doing for me. For the many "little" good things and "big" good things that happened today, I thank You. In the parts of my day when I needed to trust You a little more, I'm thankful. For the moments You surprised me with Your faithfulness, I'm grateful. For the way You poured out Your love and favor on me today, I'm humbled. I love You, Lord, no matter what. But when You surprise me with so many good things, it makes for a really, really good day! Thank You! In Jesus' name I pray, amen.

Think about it!
What good things has the Lord surprised you with today?

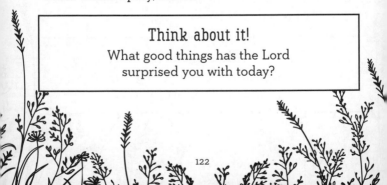

FORGIVEN

*If we confess our sins, he is faithful and
just and will forgive us our sins and
purify us from all unrighteousness.*
1 JOHN 1:9 NIV

Father God, I come to You tonight knowing I've broken some of Your rules today. Of course, I'm not perfect—everyone sins, and no one qualifies for Your glory. But I know You offer forgiveness. I just need to confess how I've sinned. And so, Lord, I will. Please search my heart. Please forgive me for my mistakes. I pray I won't fall into the same sin traps tomorrow. Help me to make right, pure choices. Help me turn away from sin. Thank You for being faithful and just. And, Lord, thank You so much for Your forgiveness! I don't deserve it, but I'm so thankful for it. In Jesus' name I pray, amen.

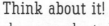

Think about it!
Have you broken any rules today that you
need to talk to Jesus about tonight?

FLAWLESS

"Every word of God is flawless; he is a shield to those who take refuge in him."

<small>PROVERBS 30:5 NIV</small>

Father God, thank You for Your Word. Thank You that it's flawless and true. Thank You that it's timeless and unchanging. I love the way it leads me. I'm thankful that it protects me—not only in the way it guides me to live a wise, holy life, but also in the way that it leads me to salvation. Instead of relying on catchy phrases or ideas that are popular in culture right now, please help me to stay firmly grounded in You and Your Word. You are my shield; and Your Word is the sword of the Spirit, the weapon I can use to defend myself every day. I pray that I'll hide Your Word in my heart and let it change my life. In Jesus' name I pray, amen.

Think about it!

What does it mean to hide God's Word in your heart?

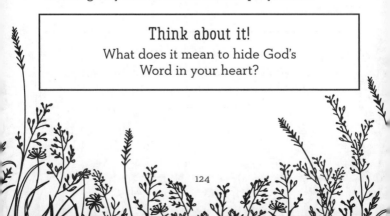

TRANSFORMED!

*Do not conform to the pattern of this world, but
be transformed by the renewing of your mind.
Then you will be able to test and approve what
God's will is—his good, pleasing and perfect will.*

ROMANS 12:2 NIV

Father God, this world and the desires and goals of
many people in it are dramatically different from You
and Your will. I pray I never try to fit into the mold
of what's "normal" or desirable in the world. Instead,
please transform me, Lord. Please renew my mind
so I can discern what Your will is. I want to do Your
will because it's good, pleasing, and perfect. I pray I'll
carefully judge my options against Your Word every
day and then choose to honor and please You with
all I think, do, and say. In Jesus' name I pray, amen.

Think about it!
What would your life be like if you
first weighed every decision, word,
and action against God's Word?

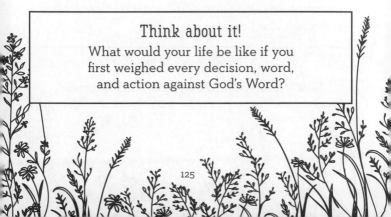

NO SHAME

*I trust in you; do not let me be put to shame,
nor let my enemies triumph over me.*
PSALM 25:2 NIV

Father, thank You for loving me, no matter what. I love that You're always here with me. Tonight, I really need some time alone with You; I need a reminder of who I am in You. I had such an embarrassing moment today. Sometimes I don't know why I act the way I do or say the things I do. And often, I get put in uncomfortable situations, and I really, really don't like it at all! Honestly, most weeks it's rare that I don't experience something super embarrassing. Regardless of what happens, please help me remember that You will *always* work things for my good. You can use all my uncomfortable, unwanted moments to transform me into a young woman who trusts You for all time. In Jesus' name I pray, amen.

Think about it!
How do you handle embarrassing moments?

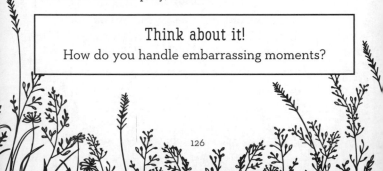

SO LONELY

*I lie awake, I have become like a
lonely bird on a housetop.*
PSALM 102:7 NASB

Father, thank You for always being with me. I know You are here, 24/7. But sometimes it's so hard to remember because I *feel* lonely. And then I try to fill that void with other things. I might try to fill it with a boyfriend, or people who I think are better, or different friends. But no human relationship will fill my loneliness—not ever. Things won't fill the hole in my heart either, Lord— not food, not shopping, not social media approval, not being busy with activities, not working hard to get good grades. . . Only You can fill the void I feel. No matter what I'm missing, only You can fill it. I pray I can rest in that tonight. In Jesus' name I pray, amen.

Think about it!
When have you tried to fill your feelings
of loneliness with a human relationship
or stuff? What was the outcome?

MY IMPERFECT BEST

Whatever you do, work at it with all your heart, as working for the Lord, not for human masters, since you know that you will receive an inheritance from the Lord as a reward. It is the Lord Christ you are serving.

Colossians 3:23–24 niv

Lord Jesus, it's an honor to serve You. I pray every day that I'll wake up and remember I'm here to work for You—and not anyone else. In all I do, I want to do my very best. I'm sorry that my best isn't perfect; in fact, I sometimes wonder if I should even try, since what I do seems so unimpressive. But please help me to remember that You never call me to perfection—because perfection is impossible for anyone but You! I'll still do things with my whole heart, though, because I do everything for You. In Your name I pray, amen.

Think about it!

How can you best serve Jesus?

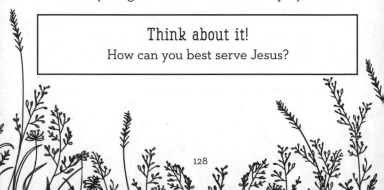

GROWING UP

Rather, speaking the truth in love, we are to grow up in every way into him who is the head, into Christ.
EPHESIANS 4:15 ESV

Father, even though I'm young and it sometimes feels like it will be *forever* before I am all grown up and on my own, I realize life does go by quickly. In fact, in many ways, it seems like my time as a little girl passed by too fast. Sometimes I think it would be nice to be a little girl again—when life was simpler, and I didn't have so many concerns and important choices to make. Please help me to remember that You'll always be my Abba Father—my Daddy! And please give me courage to grow up in You. I want to know You better every day and grow into a woman whose whole heart is set on You. In Jesus' name I pray, amen.

Think about it!
What does life look like when you
set your whole heart on Jesus?

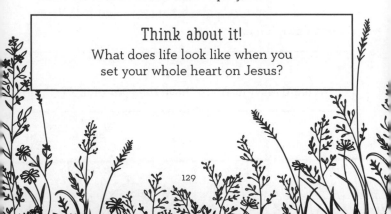

LIGHT INSTEAD OF DARKNESS

When Jesus spoke again to the people,
he said, "I am the light of the world.
Whoever follows me will never walk in
darkness, but will have the light of life."

JOHN 8:12 NIV

Lord Jesus, You are the light of the world! Because of You, I don't ever have to walk in darkness. Thank You for giving me the light of life. When darkness and fear threaten to dim my focus, help me keep my thoughts on You. Thanks for the amazing ways You light my path, Lord. If I stick with You and stop trying to do things my own selfish way, You'll lead me moment by moment. I may not know what's coming up next, but You do. And as long as I stick with You, You'll make everything clear at just the right time. This truth brings me so much comfort, and for that I'm thankful. In Your name I pray, amen.

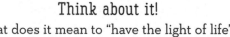

Think about it!

What does it mean to "have the light of life"?

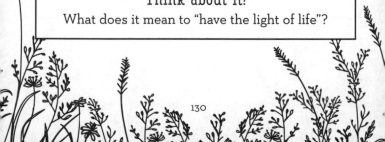

NO FEAR IN DEATH

Since the children have flesh and blood, he [Jesus] too shared in their humanity so that by his death he might break the power of him who holds the power of death—that is, the devil—and free those who all their lives were held in slavery by their fear of death.

HEBREWS 2:14–15 NIV

God, death is an awful thing. When someone close to me dies, it feels like my heart is breaking. I want to talk to, see, and hug my loved one, but I can't. You know death is awful too, Lord. You thought it was so awful that You made a way out for us—so death doesn't have the final say and it doesn't need to be feared. When You sent Jesus to earth as a man, His death and resurrection took away death's power. Thank You that everyone who has accepted the gift of Your Son's sacrifice is guaranteed life after death. There's hope. . . forever! In Jesus' name I pray, amen.

Think about it!
How does it feel to know that, if you have accepted Jesus, death isn't the final chapter?

WHOM WILL YOU SERVE?

"Now fear the LORD and serve him with all faithfulness. Throw away the gods your ancestors worshiped beyond the Euphrates River and in Egypt, and serve the LORD. But if serving the LORD seems undesirable to you, then choose for yourselves this day whom you will serve."
JOSHUA 24:14–15 NIV

Father God, the older I get, the more I want to stretch my wings and be more independent. I want to make my own decisions instead of being told what to do. I want some freedom to figure out who I really am. Yet with all of my desires to be independent, part of me also is really scared. What if I make a wrong choice? What if my decisions lead to something really bad? Please help me make choices that will glorify You and bring You honor. I choose to serve You. As long as I do that, I don't have to be afraid. And I'll know that You can use my independence and choices for You. In Jesus' name I pray, amen.

Think about it!
Why is decision-making sometimes scary? What can help with that?

MAKING FUTURE PLANS

Come now, you who say, "Today or tomorrow we will go into such and such a town and spend a year there and trade and make a profit"—yet you do not know what tomorrow will bring. What is your life? For you are a mist that appears for a little time and then vanishes. Instead you ought to say, "If the Lord wills, we will live and do this or that."

JAMES 4:13–15 ESV

Father, I'd love to know what will happen tomorrow. It's fun to imagine and prepare for what *might* happen in the days and months to come. So often, I bank a lot on my future. But I need to remember that You're in charge of tomorrow—and I am not. I'm not in control of anything! Instead of making all kinds of big plans, please help me focus just on today. Please help me to focus on serving You and accomplishing Your will for me each day. In Jesus' name I pray, amen.

Think about it!

When you dream about your future, what does your grown-up life look like?

WHY DO I NEED DISCIPLINE?

Whoever heeds discipline shows the way to life, but whoever ignores correction leads others astray.
PROVERBS 10:17 NIV

Father, I admit that I'm not a fan of discipline—in any shape or form. When I think of discipline, I think of something I've done wrong—or some strict set of rules I need to follow. But if I would stop thinking about how much I don't like the thought of discipline and instead pay attention to what You ask of me, my life would be so much better. When it comes down to it, I really don't want to ignore Your correction. Deep down, I know You discipline me because You love me and want the very best for me. Please help me remember this truth and obey Your direction. In Jesus' name I pray, amen.

Think about it!
Why is discipline important—and good?

MY LIGHT

The LORD is my light and my salvation; whom shall I fear? The LORD is the stronghold of my life; of whom shall I be afraid?

PSALM 27:1 ESV

Jesus, when You came to earth, You called Yourself the light of the world. That's exactly what You are! Just thinking of You and how much You love me lights my darkest days. I don't have to fear anything or anyone because of You. You saved me. You brighten my darkness. And I can trust You completely. When the worries of this world seem to pile up and I'm tempted to feel overwhelmed, I pray for Your peace to flood my heart. Please help me remember that I don't need to fear anything or anyone—ever. You light my way. Thank You. In Your name I pray, amen.

Think about it!
What, if any, fears do you need
to give to Jesus tonight?

FRIEND OF THE WORLD?
OR A FRIEND OF GOD?

You adulterous people! Do you not know that friendship with the world is enmity with God? Therefore whoever wishes to be a friend of the world makes himself an enemy of God.

JAMES 4:4 ESV

Father God, tonight I apologize for trying to be a friend of the world. I'm sorry for all the times I lose sight of You and Your plans and purposes. I often find my thoughts focusing on the things that don't matter: popularity, clothing, my appearance, relationships, what others think of me. . . Instead of trying to be a people pleaser, I want to please You, Lord. I don't want my thoughts to be consumed with anything other than You. I love You! I want to live a life that pleases You. And I want to be Your friend. In Jesus' name I pray, amen.

Think about it!
What does it mean to be a friend of the world?

ALWAYS WITH ME

How precious to me are your thoughts,
O God! How vast is the sum of them! If I
would count them, they are more than the
sand. I awake, and I am still with you.
PSALM 139:17–18 ESV

Father God, I'm truly amazed by You. You are so much bigger and more powerful than anything I can imagine or comprehend. And You know everything. *All things!* I praise You for Your wonderful plans that You bring to fruition in my life. I praise You for being all-knowing and always present. Thank You for never sleeping, for never letting me out of Your thoughts. No matter what I do—whether I'm sleeping or awake—I'm with You. You'll never leave me. What a comfort to my soul! I pray I'll fall asleep tonight resting in Your wonderful truth. In Jesus' name I pray, amen.

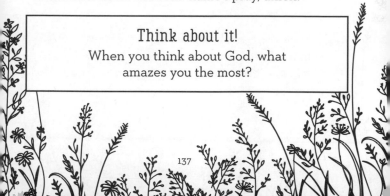

Think about it!
When you think about God, what amazes you the most?

UNDER PRESSURE

"Keep watching and praying that you may not enter into temptation; the spirit is willing, but the flesh is weak."

MATTHEW 26:41 NASB

Father, today wasn't a great day at all. Someone was pressuring me to do something I knew I shouldn't. And even though it was wrong, the temptation to do it was super appealing. As much as I knew I shouldn't give in, part of me wanted to. Under pressure like this, Father, I need You to come to my rescue. I know You'll never leave me, no matter what. And because You love me and I love You, deep down I want to make You happy. I know obedience to You will accomplish that. Please help me stand strong against temptation. I might feel weak, but with Your help, I can be strong. In Jesus' name I pray, amen.

Think about it!
When was the last time you were tempted and needed the Lord to come to your rescue?

WALK IN LOVE

*And walk in love, as Christ loved us
and gave himself up for us, a fragrant
offering and sacrifice to God.*

EPHESIANS 5:2 ESV

Father, when Jesus was on earth, He commanded His disciples to love each other as He loved them. I know I need to love others. And sometimes I *want* to love other people, but other times I really, truly don't. I need Your help! Tomorrow, please open my eyes and show me how I can walk in Your love. I'll admit that it feels like a sacrifice to love people I don't want to love—or to love people who I don't think deserve my love. Please help me love them anyway. Give me eyes to notice those around me who need Your love; and then give me the strength and courage to love them well. In Jesus' name I pray, amen.

Think about it!
What is your favorite way to show
God's love to others?

SHOW ME THE WAY

"I am the LORD your God, who teaches you what is best for you, who directs you in the way you should go. If only you had paid attention to my commands, your peace would have been like a river, your well-being like the waves of the sea."
ISAIAH 48:17–18 NIV

Father, You always know what's happening—You know what *has* happened, what *is* happening, and what *will* happen in the future. I love that You have a plan, not just for the world, but for my life too. Knowing that You have a plan for my future helps me fully rest in You. Sometimes I feel afraid because I think I'm not doing the right things; or I get confused when I need to make important choices that will affect my life in a big way. I want to pay attention to Your commands and do Your will. Lord, I'm willing. Please use me. I can't wait to see what You have in store for me! In Jesus' name I pray, amen.

Think about it!
If God truly has everything under His control, do you ever need to worry about a single thing?

BECOMING A PEACEMAKER

*"Blessed are the peacemakers, for they
will be called children of God."*
MATTHEW 5:9 NIV

Lord, You brought peace to this world. And You've brought peace to me! I pray I would model Your peace wherever I go. Please help me to live peacefully with the people around me. Instead of stirring up trouble, I want to be a calming influence. Even when people would rather lash out in anger or hate, help me to give a peaceful response. While my peace may not be well received, I can—and should—still try. Like You, I can offer peace in every situation. At the end of the day, I'll gladly take Your peace with a thankful heart. I love You, Jesus. In Your name I pray, amen.

Think about it!

Is it easy or difficult for you to remain calm when others lash out? What can you do or say to bring calm to a chaotic situation?

HELP!

*In my distress I called upon the LORD, and
cried to my God for help; He heard my
voice out of His temple, and my cry for
help before Him came into His ears.*
PSALM 18:6 NASB

My Lord and my God, I need Your help. You know
what's going on. I want to change what has happened;
and honestly, I'm afraid of what might happen next. I
don't want to live in fear, though. And I don't want to
live a life of regret. So, Lord, please come to my rescue.
Thank You for hearing me. Thank You for knowing
what I need before I speak a word—even when I have
no words to describe what I'm thinking and feeling.
I'm so thankful for You and the way I can trust You
completely. In Jesus' name I pray, amen.

Think about it!
When you're struggling, who do you talk
to first? Who *should* you talk to first?

WHAT I DON'T HAVE

The LORD will give strength to His people;
the LORD will bless His people with peace.

PSALM 29:11 NASB

Father God, tonight I have so much on my mind. Even though it feels like my thoughts are weighing me down, I'm so thankful that You can replace my worries with peace. You have a way of blessing me with peace like nothing, and no one, else—and for that, I'm glad. I'm also thankful that You give strength. I know my weaknesses; but amazingly, Your power is perfected in my weakness. When I'm weak, You make me strong. It's incredible that You can take what I'm lacking and turn it into something miraculous. When I'm feeling discouraged, I pray that You'll help me to keep my eyes on You and remember that You alone can help. I'm so thankful for You and Your peace and strength! In Jesus' name I pray, amen.

Think about it!
In what areas are you the weakest? Where do you most need God's strength?

ONE STEP AT A TIME

*Ponder the path of your feet; then all your
ways will be sure. Do not swerve to the right
or to the left; turn your foot away from evil.*

PROVERBS 4:26–27 ESV

Father, thank You for today. I give tomorrow to You.
Please use me how You'd like. I'm all Yours. As I make
life's little and big decisions, help me think through
the best way to go. I don't want to just wander around
aimlessly reacting to whatever comes my way. I want
to stay on the right path—the one You've planned
for me. And I can't do that without Your help. Please
steer me away from evil. I want to live in a way that
shows others Your truth and beauty. Please make my
footsteps—and all my choices—sure and firm. In Jesus'
name I pray, amen.

Think about it!
Do you regularly ask for God's help and guidance
before making a decision? Why or why not?

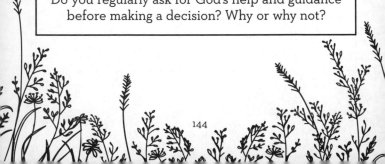

FREEDOM!

Live as people who are free, not using your freedom as a cover-up for evil, but living as servants of God.
1 PETER 2:16 ESV

Heavenly Father, thank You for freedom that comes through Jesus. I don't have to live as a slave to the law. I don't have to try to earn salvation on my own. I can't save myself, no matter what I do. Instead of feeling bad about that, I'm thankful because You've given me freedom. Thank You for saving me! As I enjoy my freedom in Christ, I pray that I won't use it as an excuse to sin and then follow up with an immediate request for forgiveness afterward. Instead, I want to live as Your servant. I don't want to waste my freedom, take it for granted, or misuse it. Please help me treat it as the incredible gift that it is. In Jesus' name I pray, amen.

Think about it!
What does it mean to have freedom in Christ?

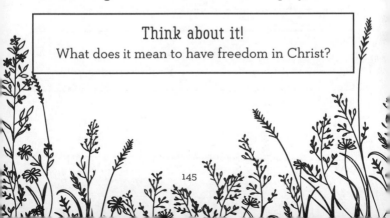

LOVE IS THE ANSWER

"You have heard that it was said, 'Love your neighbor and hate your enemy.' But I tell you, love your enemies and pray for those who persecute you, that you may be children of your Father in heaven."
MATTHEW 5:43–45 NIV

Lord Jesus, Your instruction to love my enemies and pray for those who persecute me is so difficult to follow. It doesn't feel natural to love people who hurt me and mistreat me. But, Father, I trust You. I want to obey You. So, as difficult as it is, please help me love the people who are hardest to love. When I'm tempted to react negatively out of hurt and fear, please help me to choose love instead. Help me fight against what comes naturally—hating my enemy—and to be different from the world around me. Help me to live like I am a child of my Father in heaven. In Jesus' name I pray, amen.

Think about it!
Why is it sometimes so difficult to choose love?

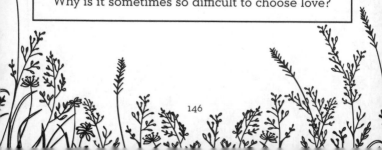

THREE STUMBLING BLOCKS

For all that is in the world—the desires of the flesh and the desires of the eyes and pride of life—is not from the Father but is from the world. And the world is passing away along with its desires, but whoever does the will of God abides forever.

1 JOHN 2:16–17 ESV

God, it's easy to be swayed by the world: the desires of my flesh, the desires of my eyes, the pride of life. Everything that tempts me, and so often consumes my thoughts, falls into those three categories. Am I obsessing over relationships or how someone else can make me feel? Am I stuck thinking about all my wants? Am I proud of myself and all the things I can do? Please help me remember that none of it is important. Everything apart from You won't last. I don't want to be stuck dwelling on the things that aren't important or of value. In Jesus' name I pray, amen.

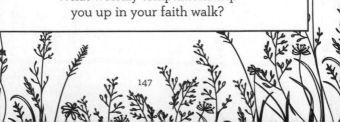

Think about it!
What worldly temptations trip
you up in your faith walk?

SET APART

It is God's will that you should be sanctified: that you should avoid sexual immorality; that each of you should learn to control your own body in a way that is holy and honorable, not in passionate lust like the pagans, who do not know God. . . . For God did not call us to be impure, but to live a holy life.

1 THESSALONIANS 4:3–5, 7 NIV

Father, so much in this world elevates immorality as a good thing. People use their influence to try to talk me into thinking or doing things that would compromise my purity. It's difficult to fight against the temptation. But, Father, I want to follow You—to obey Your call for me to stay pure in both my body and my mind. Although it's tempting to give in under pressure, Father, I trust You'll give me the strength and wisdom to make the best choices for my life. In Jesus' name I pray, amen.

Think about it!
Are you easily influenced by the world? Why or why not?

WALK IN THE LIGHT

*Let no one deceive you with empty words,
for because of these things the wrath of God
comes upon the sons of disobedience. Therefore
do not become partners with them; for at
one time you were darkness, but now you are
light in the Lord. Walk as children of light.*

EPHESIANS 5:6–8 ESV

Father God, I don't want to be deceived! I don't want
to fall into a trap of lies. Instead, I want to walk in Your
light and Your truth. I pray I'll make choices that honor
You. Please help me be careful about who I choose to
spend time with. I want to be a light to people living in
darkness. I pray that while I'm living in this world, I'll
be set apart—not acting like I'm holier than everyone
else, but making obedient choices that please You. In
Jesus' name I pray, amen.

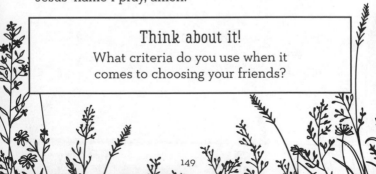

Think about it!
What criteria do you use when it
comes to choosing your friends?

THE POWER OF CHOICE

God "will repay each person according to what they have done." To those who by persistence in doing good seek glory, honor and immortality, he will give eternal life. But for those who are self-seeking and who reject the truth and follow evil, there will be wrath and anger.

ROMANS 2:6–8 NIV

Father, it's easy to make a choice in the heat of the moment and forget that it comes with consequences. Please help me remember that You'll repay me according to what I do in this life. I want to bring You glory in all I do. I want to live by the power of Your Holy Spirit. Please help me live like every moment matters. I want to know Your truth and follow it. I want Your truth to be evident in my life. Please help me keep my eyes on You. In Jesus' name I pray, amen.

Think about it!
What's the best choice you ever made and why? What about your worst?

LIVING IN PEACE

*Make every effort to live in peace
with everyone and to be holy.*
HEBREWS 12:14 NIV

Lord, You know how difficult it is to live in peace with everyone! Some people are just difficult to get along with, and some people love to stir up trouble. I don't want to be like those people, Lord. As much as it's in my control, I want to be a peacemaker. Please help me live in peace with my friends, family, neighbors. . . and even strangers. Help me to bring peace to tense situations instead of stirring up more trouble. I want to live a holy life. And a holy life includes showing the world Your love and hope. Father, I pray that I can do that by bringing peace to people's lives. In Jesus' name I pray, amen.

Think about it!

What are some ways you can be a peacemaker?

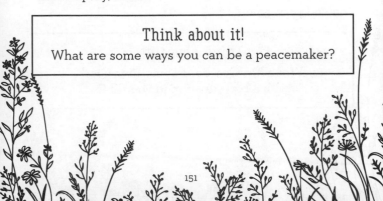

INTENDED FOR GOOD

But Joseph said to them, "Don't be afraid. Am I in the place of God? You intended to harm me, but God intended it for good to accomplish what is now being done, the saving of many lives."

GENESIS 50:19–20 NIV

Father, I love the way You redeem what seems utterly hopeless in this world. You can turn things around and make things right that seem all wrong. Just like You used Joseph's awful situation in Egypt to save so many people, You're also working things out for good in my life today. When people intend to harm me, You'll use those moments for good. You'll always accomplish Your will in my life and in the world, no matter what. For that, I'm grateful. And because of Your goodness, I can fall asleep in peace. In Jesus' name I pray, amen.

Think about it!
When has God done something good
with a bad situation in your life?

UNDER THE WEATHER

Is anyone among you sick? Let them call the elders of the church to pray over them and anoint them with oil in the name of the Lord. And the prayer offered in faith will make the sick person well; the Lord will raise them up. If they have sinned, they will be forgiven. Therefore confess your sins to each other and pray for each other so that you may be healed. The prayer of a righteous person is powerful and effective.

JAMES 5:14–16 NIV

Heavenly Father, You're the Great Physician and healer. As much as I know these truths, I'm still worried when a loved one gets sick. Please comfort those who are ill, Lord. Ease their pain and worries. Whether You decide to heal them here on earth or in heaven, give them grace and peace. Help me to be an encouragement too. Show me how I can help in any way. I trust You completely. In Jesus' name I pray, amen.

Think about it!

How can you best encourage someone who is sick?

153

YOU DESERVE PRAISE!

*Every day I will bless you and praise your name
forever and ever. Great is the Lord, and greatly
to be praised, and his greatness is unsearchable.*
PSALM 145:2–3 ESV

Lord God, You are great! You are mighty! You're so
worthy of praise, and I'll never know the full extent
of Your majesty and greatness. Tonight, I praise Your
name. Thank You for all You've done in my life and
heart—and thank You for continuing to work in me
and through me. When I think of every challenge
and disappointment I have faced, You were there.
As I think about the wonderful moments You have
brought into my life, You were there for each one! You
are faithful. You are good. And I'm thankful You've
chosen me as Your daughter. When I'm distracted
by the world, please bring my focus back to You. In
Jesus' name I pray, amen.

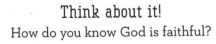

Think about it!
How do you know God is faithful?

TOMORROW'S A NEW DAY

Sing the praises of the LORD, you his faithful people; praise his holy name. For his anger lasts only a moment, but his favor lasts a lifetime; weeping may stay for the night, but rejoicing comes in the morning.

PSALM 30:4-5 NIV

Lord, I praise You! You are holy. There is nothing—and no one else—like You in all of creation. I thank You for Your love and Your favor. I couldn't earn either of them on my own. And yet, You've chosen me! Thank You for forgiving my sin and giving me the undeserved gift of Your grace. Even when I go to bed sad and exhausted after a long, emotional day, I am thankful that I can wake up to a fresh start. Though I may feel heartbroken tonight, You can—*and will*—fill me with joy again tomorrow. Thank You. In Jesus' name I pray, amen.

Think about it!
Why are fresh starts so important?

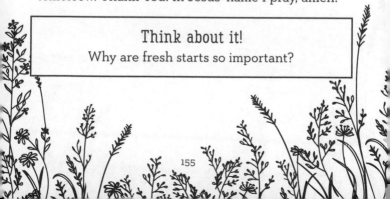

THINGS OF THE WORLD

What I mean, brothers and sisters, is that the time is short. From now on. . .those who buy something, [should live] as if it were not theirs to keep; those who use the things of the world, as if not engrossed in them. For this world in its present form is passing away.

1 CORINTHIANS 7:29–31 NIV

Father, it's so easy for me to get distracted by the world and to let it consume my time, energy, and thoughts. I don't want that to be the case for me, though, and I don't want to measure my success by the world's standards. Please help me keep my focus on You. I am rejoicing tonight because I don't have to work for Your approval. When You see me, You see me as forgiven and accepted through Jesus' loving sacrifice. I am so grateful! In Jesus' name I pray, amen.

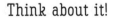

Think about it!

What is the best way to measure your success?

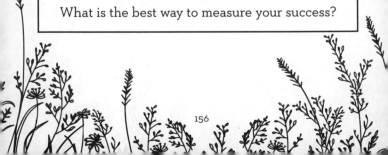

GOOD VS. EVIL

For it is better, if it is God's will, to suffer
for doing good than for doing evil.
1 PETER 3:17 NIV

Father, I want to do Your will, no matter what. Even though I sometimes feel so pressured to do wrong by people around me, I want to please You more than anyone else. Would You please give me strength to follow Your commands and live like Your daughter? Help me make the right decisions instead of choosing sinful ones. Even if people make fun of me, purposely overlook me, or try to harm me, I trust You'll always protect me and remind me that I am loved and that I am Yours. You are the ultimate judge. You are the one true God. In Jesus' name I pray, amen.

Think about it!
Why do you think people sometimes pressure others to do wrong?

ALL MY NEEDS

*And my God will supply all your needs according
to His riches in glory in Christ Jesus.*

PHILIPPIANS 4:19 NASB

Father, I'm worried. I wonder what is coming next
and how You'll provide for me. What will happen
in school? What career should I pursue? What will
happen with my family? Who are my true friends?
Who should I date? Will I get married? . . . For all
the uncertainty, I praise You for being my provider.
You're my Jehovah-jireh—the God who supplies all
my needs. More than anything, I want to rest in the
truth that You will provide all my needs according
to Your riches. Help me remember that the riches of
Your glory are truly amazing. Thank You for blessing
me with my needs—and even some of my wants! I fully
trust You. In Jesus' name I pray, amen.

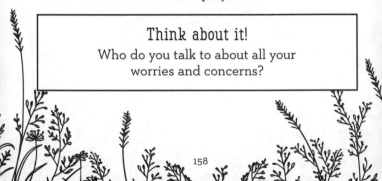

Think about it!
Who do you talk to about all your
worries and concerns?

MAKING THE MOST OF EVERY OPPORTUNITY

Be very careful, then, how you live—not as unwise but as wise, making the most of every opportunity, because the days are evil.
EPHESIANS 5:15–16 NIV

Lord Jesus, I want to be careful about how I live. So, it's important that I thoroughly consider my day-to-day decisions. Please help me live wisely. Help me to realize that all the little choices I make add up. Every day is filled with little (and big!) opportunities to follow You, obey what You command, and share Your love with the world around me. Please help me be a good witness and example for You in the words I speak, my attitudes, and my actions. Show me all the opportunities You have for me, Father—and help me boldly use them for You. Please help me share Your love with those who need it the most. In Jesus' name I pray, amen.

Think about it!
How can you be sure you're making the most of every opportunity God sends your way?

HUNGER AND THIRST NO MORE

Then Jesus declared, "I am the bread of life.
Whoever comes to me will never go hungry, and
whoever believes in me will never be thirsty."
JOHN 6:35 NIV

Lord Jesus, I am so glad You are the bread of life. You alone satisfy hunger like nothing else can. You meet all my needs, not only physically but also spiritually—and for that I'm so thankful. Please help me to stop trying to find fulfillment and satisfaction in the things of this world. Instead, I want to live in freedom because You've given me everything I need. I don't need to worry about this life or the one to come, because life is found in You and only You. I'm thankful for the way You satisfy my soul completely. In Your name I pray, amen.

Think about it!
How does God provide for you both
physically and spiritually?

PEACE WITH YOU

Therefore, since we have been justified through faith, we have peace with God through our Lord Jesus Christ.

ROMANS 5:1 NIV

Heavenly Father, I would love to experience peace tonight, here in my little corner of the world. You want me to experience peace too! But it's impossible for me to have true peace unless it comes from You. Thank You for sending Jesus. Thank You that He came to give peace—not as the world gives, but only as He could give. His peace isn't something that just involves the absence of bad things, like fighting; His peace means the presence of something *really* good. Through Jesus, I've gained a serene, peaceful heart that I don't have to work for or earn—I have His peace because I am His and He is mine. Thank You for peace that satisfies more than anything else in the world. In Jesus' name I pray, amen.

Think about it!

Why is the peace of Jesus so special and unique?

WHAT CAN COMPARE?

You have multiplied, O LORD my God, your
wondrous deeds and your thoughts toward us;
none can compare with you! I will proclaim and
tell of them, yet they are more than can be told.
PSALM 40:5 ESV

Father, I'm amazed by You and Your creation.
Everything that has breath lives because of You. You
are all-knowing. You have a perfect plan for me—even
if I don't understand what that plan is. But I don't need
to understand to worship You and praise You for who
You are and all You do. Nothing—and no one—in this
world compares to You. Your power is mind-boggling.
The mercy You've shown me is undeserved and so
kind, and I am so grateful! I pray that I'll naturally want
to tell people about You and the good things You've
done for me. In Jesus' name I pray, amen.

Think about it!

Does anything or anyone compare to Jesus?

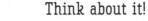

JUST ASK

If any of you lacks wisdom, you should ask God, who gives generously to all without finding fault, and it will be given to you.

JAMES 1:5 NIV

Father God, I'm so confused. I sometimes don't know what to do day to day, but especially when it comes to future plans. There is so much uncertainty. I don't know what Your will is for me and my life. I pray for wisdom! Please give me clear thoughts and help me to make wise decisions. I want to honor You with my choices. Thank You for giving generously in everything, but especially when it comes to wisdom. I pray You'll guide me and that I'll pay attention when You nudge me. As I look to You and Your Word for guidance, please make the wise choices clear to me. I pray my soul will find rest as I trust You to lead me. In Jesus' name I pray, amen.

Think about it!
What choices cause you the most confusion and uncertainty?

THE TREASURE OF WISDOM

How much better to get wisdom than gold! To get understanding is to be chosen rather than silver.
PROVERBS 16:16 ESV

Father, people often focus on money and belongings. According to Your Word, it's always been that way; but it seems like even more so today, people really obsess over their possessions. I don't want to fall into that trap. When some of my friends get the newest and best of everything, I pray I won't become envious. Please help me remember that certain things—like wisdom and understanding—are better than riches. I ask that You would fill me with Your wisdom and understanding. I know I won't suddenly become wise overnight, but please help me make wise decisions every day until I have a much better understanding of life. In Jesus' name I pray, amen.

Think about it!
What is better than riches?

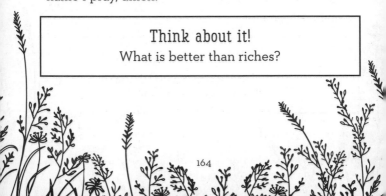

MY HIDING PLACE

*You are my hiding place; you will
protect me from trouble.*

PSALM 32:7 NIV

Father God, I love that You are my hiding place. This means that when bad things are happening all around me, I can always find shelter in You. You protect me from trouble like nothing or no one else can. And if—or when—I get hurt, You'll always be a strong and sure place for me. I'm so glad I can run into Your open arms. I trust that You'll teach me the way I should go and gently counsel me with love and kindness. Thank You that You are *for* me and not against me. In Jesus' name I pray, amen.

Think about it!
Who is your best protector?

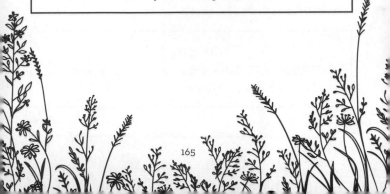

LIVING IN AN UNBELIEVING WORLD

*If you are insulted because of the name
of Christ, you are blessed, for the Spirit
of glory and of God rests on you.*

1 PETER 4:14 NIV

God, You know what kind of pressures I face. You're fully aware that people in this world hate You and say horrible, untrue things about You. Comments that I hear about You and Your followers make me feel sick to my stomach. Ugly words reveal what's inside people's hearts. These people desperately need You to save them. Please remind me that every insult directed my way for being Your follower means that I'm not of this world. There's *more* to this life. Thank You that Your Spirit of glory rests on me and makes me stand apart from unbelievers. I find my hope in You alone. In Jesus' name I pray, amen.

Think about it!
When unbelievers speak untruths about
God, how should you respond?

LIFE IS GOOD

Surely your goodness and love will follow
me all the days of my life, and I will dwell
in the house of the LORD forever.

PSALM 23:6 NIV

Lord, every day is a gift—even the bad days. But on most bad days, it's hard to recognize Your gifts. Please open my eyes to all the beauty around me and all the amazing things You're doing for my benefit—whether I'm having a good or bad day. I know that, regardless of what happens each day, Your goodness and love always follow me. Wherever I go, whatever I do, You're surprising me with Your good gifts. Thank You! Thank You for adding joy to my life. I'm so happy knowing that one day You'll welcome me into heaven to live with You forever. That will be more incredible than I can ever imagine. I love You. In Jesus' name I pray, amen.

Think about it!
How can a bad day be a "gift"?

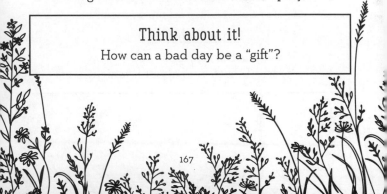

LIVING LIKE I'M YOUNG

Flee the evil desires of youth and pursue righteousness, faith, love and peace, along with those who call on the Lord out of a pure heart.
2 TIMOTHY 2:22 NIV

Father, I get tired of feeling like I'm less of a person because of my age. I know You value my life, and I know You have wonderful plans for me. But Your Word also clearly says that young people don't always make the wisest choices. If I'm supposed to flee the evil desires of youth, that means my heart will be pulled in a direction that doesn't bring You honor. Please give me wisdom to know the difference between right and wrong, good and evil. Help me pursue righteousness, faith, love, and peace. I want to live a life of abundant faith. I want to share Your love with the world. In Jesus' name I pray, amen.

Think about it!
What has the strongest pull on your heart? Talk to God about it tonight.

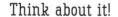

THINK ABOUT THIS. . .

Finally, brothers and sisters, whatever is true, whatever is noble, whatever is right, whatever is pure, whatever is lovely, whatever is admirable—if anything is excellent or praiseworthy—think about such things.

PHILIPPIANS 4:8 NIV

Lord, sometimes it's hard to think about good things. Surrounded by the muck of this world, it's hard to focus on what's true and beautiful. The line between right and wrong is often blurry. Purity? . . . It appears to be vanishing from the world around me. And things that are lovely, admirable, excellent, and praiseworthy can also be very hard to find. Father, I pray that I might find good things in the everyday moments of life. Help me delight in what's true, noble, right, pure, lovely, admirable, excellent, and praiseworthy. I'd love to be surprised by these things daily—and celebrate them as wonderful gifts from You. In Jesus' name I pray, amen.

Think about it!
What good and lovely things did you notice today?

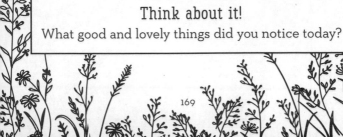

FAITH AND BELIEF

This righteousness is given through faith
in Jesus Christ to all who believe.
ROMANS 3:22 NIV

Father God, thank You for Jesus! Thank You that because of my faith in Jesus Christ, I can be made right with You. My faith is a very real thing I can possess or receive—it's a lot like receiving a present. When I'm presented a gift, it's not truly mine until I accept it and make it my own. I must take the gift from the giver and open it up. It's the same with my faith. Jesus isn't truly mine until I accept Him and make Him my own. I choose to believe today—I choose the gift of Jesus. I trust that Your righteousness will be given to me through faith. In Jesus' name I pray, amen.

Think about it!
How is faith in Jesus like a gift?

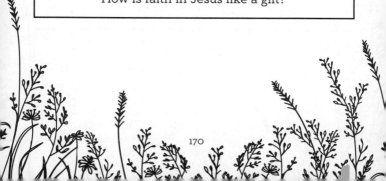

PEACEFUL SLEEP

In peace I will lie down and sleep, for you alone, LORD, make me dwell in safety.

PSALM 4:8 NIV

Heavenly Father, You are a God of peace. In fact, You are *the* peace giver; and so, tonight, I will lie down and sleep without fear or worry. You're my great protector. I don't have to worry what might happen tomorrow or in the months to come, because I know You'll prepare the way. I don't have to toss and turn all night because You make me dwell in safety. Your protection and safety and peace are such wonderful—and needed— gifts. Thank You, Lord! Thank You for freeing me from fear. Thank You for the gift of sweet, peaceful sleep that restores my energy and revives my spirit. You are so good to me. In the name of Jesus, the Prince of Peace, I pray, amen.

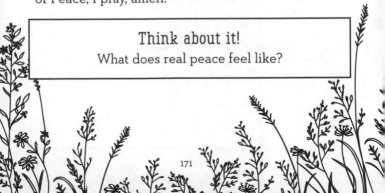

Think about it!
What does real peace feel like?

NEVER FORGET

"Can a mother forget the baby at her breast and have no compassion on the child she has borne? Though she may forget, I will not forget you! See, I have engraved you on the palms of my hands."

ISAIAH 49:15–16 NIV

Lord Jesus, no matter what happens in my life, I always want to remember certain people. But as much as I want to remember people who are special to me, sometimes the human brain doesn't work as well as it should, and people are forgotten. I am so thankful that You don't ever forget me, Lord. No matter what, You've promised to remember me—and You've always kept that promise. It's evident in the work You do in and through my life. Knowing that I matter so much to You amazes me. Thank You for loving me and caring about me as only You can. In Your name I pray, amen.

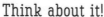

Think about it!
How do you know that God never forgets you?

LISTEN AND DO

Do not merely listen to the word, and so
deceive yourselves. Do what it says.
JAMES 1:22 NIV

Lord God, Your Word is true. It's living and active. It can judge my thoughts and my heart's intentions. Your Word can even guide me—if I'll let it. I thank You for the gift of Your Word. I pray I won't forget it. I pray I won't just read it and then choose to do my own thing. I want to obey. . .to do what Your Word asks. As it guides me, please give me strength and courage to follow everything it says. I want You to direct my life. Please help me know and understand what Your Word says, use it as the foundation of my life, and then put it into action—even if it seems difficult. In Jesus' name I pray, amen.

Think about it!
How should you interact with God's Word?

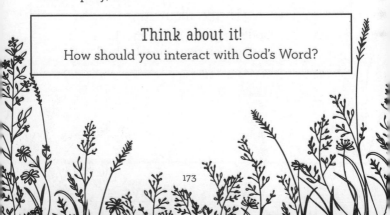

LAUGHING AT THE FUTURE

She is clothed with strength and dignity;
she can laugh at the days to come.
PROVERBS 31:25 NIV

Father, because I fully trust in You, I don't ever have to worry about my future. In fact, I can laugh at the days that will come. When people around me are stressed out with the turmoil in the world or are worried about what they should do, I can rejoice and rest in You. You give me strength. You give me courage. And, as I trust in You, You clothe me with dignity so that I'm worthy of honor and respect. Thank You! Knowing that I have nothing to fear is a big deal! And feeling the strength You give me is such a comfort. You are so good to me, and I'm forever grateful. In Jesus' name I pray, amen.

Think about it!
God has given you so much.
What are you most grateful for?

PRAISE THE LORD!

I will bless the LORD at all times; his praise shall continually be in my mouth.

PSALM 34:1 ESV

Father God, You have a plan for all of time and eternity. Nothing escapes Your notice, and nothing surprises You. Even when I feel like I don't have much faith, still You are faithful. Even when I feel like I don't have much love, still You are loving. Even when sin separated humans from Your perfection, still You made a way of forgiveness and mercy through Jesus. Thank You! I praise You tonight because You are good even when my circumstances are not. You comfort and guide me even when times are tough. When I have an amazing day, You give all good things. Your awesomeness is more than I can comprehend. In Jesus' name I pray, amen.

Think about it!
How awesome is God?

175

WHAT IS LOVE?

Love is patient and kind; love does not envy or boast; it is not arrogant or rude. It does not insist on its own way; it is not irritable or resentful; it does not rejoice at wrongdoing, but rejoices with the truth. Love bears all things, believes all things, hopes all things, endures all things. Love never ends.

1 CORINTHIANS 13:4–8 ESV

Father, Your love has changed the world. It has also changed my heart and my life. When I think of Your love, my love doesn't even come close. Jesus said people would know His followers by their love. And He demonstrated how to love others well. I want to be like Jesus. I want to love others exceptionally well, and I want to be known by my love—for others and for You! Please fill me with Your Holy Spirit, and let Your love spill out of me to everyone around me. In Jesus' name I pray, amen.

Think about it!
How can you love others like Jesus loves?

WHERE DOES MY HELP COME FROM?

I lift up my eyes to the mountains—where does my help come from? My help comes from the LORD, the Maker of heaven and earth. He will not let your foot slip—he who watches over you will not slumber.

PSALM 121:1–3 NIV

Lord, I am so thankful that You never quit. And You never stop watching out for me. Thank You for Your nonstop love! Thank You for protecting me. You never sleep, so You're always aware of what's going on in my life and in the whole universe. I'm amazed by Your creation—the mountains, the oceans, every single person, heaven, and all of earth. And even though that's a lot to take care of, You still love and care for me. You are worthy of all my honor and praise, Lord. I love You! In Jesus' name I pray, amen.

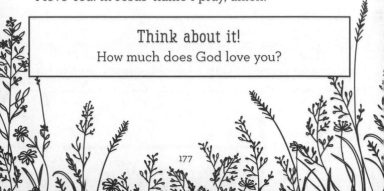

Think about it!
How much does God love you?

CONTENTMENT!

But godliness with contentment is great gain.
For we brought nothing into the world, and we
can take nothing out of it. But if we have food
and clothing, we will be content with that.

1 TIMOTHY 6:6–8 NIV

Father God, I really want to be content with all You've given me. It's so easy to get caught up in thinking about things I wish I had and all the things I don't have. Why do I always want more? Why do I always want something different? Instead of thinking about things—clothes and belongings and what I want to eat—please help me focus on being more like You. When I'm more like You, I become more content. And when I become more like You, I can make an impact on the world that lasts! Thank You, Lord! In Jesus' name I pray, amen.

Think about it!

How can you change your thinking to become more content with what you already have?

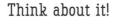

HONOR

*"Honor your father and mother"—which is
the first commandment with a promise—"so
that it may go well with you and that you
may enjoy long life on the earth."*

EPHESIANS 6:2–3 NIV

Father, sometimes I get so angry with my parents. I
don't always understand why You chose this family for
me. Even though I get frustrated, please help me see
all the ways Mom and Dad are a blessing to me. Help
them to better understand me and where I'm coming
from. Help me to understand them and where they're
coming from too. I know You want me to honor my
parents. And I know I should. Please help me, Lord.
I want to appreciate all my parents do for me. I truly
want to learn from them. In Jesus' name I pray, amen.

Think about it!

How can you better honor your father and mother?

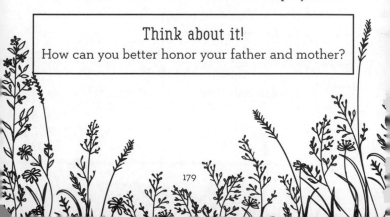

FEARLESS

"So have no fear of them, for nothing is covered that will not be revealed, or hidden that will not be known. What I tell you in the dark, say in the light, and what you hear whispered, proclaim on the housetops. And do not fear those who kill the body but cannot kill the soul."

MATTHEW 10:26–28 ESV

Jesus, when You lived on earth, You knew what was in the hearts of men. Yet, You didn't fear them. You, as the Son of God, knew that even if men could kill Your body, they couldn't kill Your soul. I'm thankful You didn't live in fear—and because of Your sacrifice for me, I don't need to live in fear either. Please help me boldly live for You. Please use my mouth, my mind, and my hands to point others to You. Help me proclaim Your truth and Your teachings to the world—without fear! In Your name I pray, amen.

Think about it!

How is your "fearless level" tonight?
Do you need to ask God for more courage?

I'M YOUR GIRL

The LORD called me from the womb, from the body of my mother he named my name.

ISAIAH 49:1 ESV

Father God, I'm Your girl. Your Word says so! In fact, You've known me since *before* I was even created. You made me wonderfully well. You called me from my mother's womb. You chose me. . .You delight in me. This is so amazing and hard to imagine! It's unbelievable, really. And sometimes I wonder *why*. Why me? I'll never know the answer, but You do, Lord. Thank You. Thank You for creating me. Thank You for calling me. Thank You for naming me. Thank You for choosing me as Your very own. I'm forever grateful. In Jesus' name I pray, amen.

> ## Think about it!
> If you're chosen by God, what is your worth?

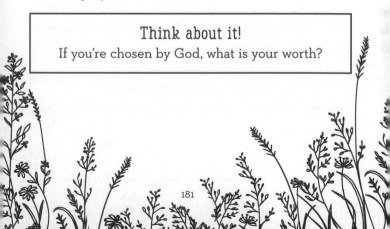

VANISHED!

As far as the east is from the west, so far does he remove our transgressions from us.

PSALM 103:12 ESV

Lord, You know my sins. Tonight, I come to You in need of forgiveness. I confess the wrong I've done. Instead of living with the burden of my mistakes, please help me to readily accept Your mercy and grace. Knowing that You completely remove my sins astounds me. They've vanished! You've removed them as far as the east is from the west—and it really doesn't get any farther than that, does it! Thank You for Your forgiveness. Please help me turn from my sin and walk instead toward Your light. Through the power of Your Holy Spirit, please help me live in obedience to You. I want to please You. I want to be a good representative of You in everything I say and do. In Jesus' name I pray, amen.

Think about it!
How big is God's forgiveness?

DOING WHAT'S RIGHT

For what credit is there if, when you sin and are harshly treated, you endure it with patience? But if when you do what is right and suffer for it you patiently endure it, this finds favor with God.

1 PETER 2:20 NASB

God, it's difficult to make decisions between right and wrong every single day. I wish right choices would already be made for me! But life in this world is not like that. And so, I pray You'll help me know what's right to do—and then help me follow through. I want to do what's right and good, no matter what. Even if people make fun of me or try to make my life miserable, I still want to do what's right. I need Your help to do this. Although it will be hard, it will be so worth it! I know it's what You want me to do. In Jesus' name I pray, amen.

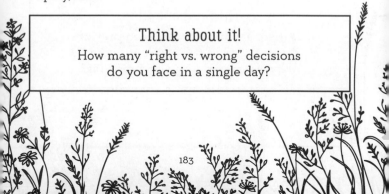

Think about it!

How many "right vs. wrong" decisions
do you face in a single day?

WAITING FOR YOU

I waited patiently for the LORD;
he turned to me and heard my cry.
PSALM 40:1 NIV

Father, thank You for hearing my prayers. Thank You for being worthy of being prayed to. I love that I can trust You. And I love that You have the best plans in mind for me. I want to be honest, though. I've been praying about something for a long time. You know what it is, Lord. I keep praying because it's so important to me. Please help me be patient as I wait for You to answer. I know Your answer might be yes—or it might be no. Or it might be to wait. Oh, the waiting is hard! But no matter what Your answer is, and especially in the waiting, I will put all my trust in You. I love You! In Jesus' name I pray, amen.

Think about it!

Is there anything you've been praying about—and God still hasn't answered? Why is it important to keep praying?

WE ARE FAMILY

But to all who did receive him, who believed in his name, he gave the right to become children of God, who were born, not of blood nor of the will of the flesh nor of the will of man, but of God.
JOHN 1:12–13 ESV

Father God, I am so thankful You've invited me—and others—to become Your children. Even though not everyone says yes, You've still sent the invitation to everyone. I'll gladly accept, Lord! I receive Christ; I believe in His name. And I'm so thankful that I'm born of You—as Your child. . .Your daughter. I didn't earn this on my own. My status as Your daughter didn't depend on my family tree. No. It's Your will, and Yours alone. It's Your amazing gift to me. Thank You! I am glad to be part of Your family. In Jesus' name I pray, amen.

Think about it!
What does it mean to be part of God's family?

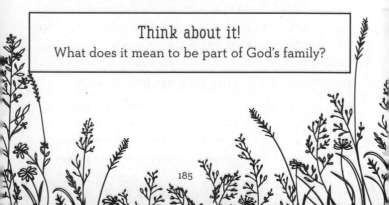

BE CHOOSY

My dear brothers and sisters, take note of this: Everyone should be quick to listen, slow to speak and slow to become angry, because human anger does not produce the righteousness that God desires.

JAMES 1:19–20 NIV

Lord, please keep watch over my mouth. It's so easy to blurt out what I'm thinking. Or worse, sometimes I start talking without giving one thought to my words. It can be embarrassing when the words escape my lips—and I can't take them back. Please help me to be a better listener—I want to be quick to listen instead of only planning my response. I pray that as I listen, I wouldn't make quick judgments or reactions. Please help me be slow when it comes to getting angry. Please help me keep my tongue and emotions in check. It's hard, but through You and Your power, it's possible. In Your name I pray, amen.

Think about it!
When was the last time you spoke without thinking? What were the consequences?

THE AUTHOR OF MY STORY

Your eyes have seen my unformed substance;
and in Your book were all written the
days that were ordained for me, when
as yet there was not one of them.
PSALM 139:16 NASB

Father, You are amazing. You created all things. You know all things. You've written the story of my life. And even though certain parts of my story don't always make sense—in my mind, anyway—You weave it all together into one beautiful life. You've known me since before I was born. No detail of my life has escaped Your notice. And as much as I'd like to know what's in store for me or why certain things have happened—or not happened—I choose to trust You as the master storyteller. Thank You for knowing everything about me and choosing to love me despite my weaknesses. In Jesus' name I pray, amen.

Think about it!
How would you title the story of your life? Why?

FOCUS ON THE GOOD

Rejoice always, pray without ceasing, give thanks in all circumstances; for this is the will of God in Christ Jesus for you.

1 Thessalonians 5:16–18 esv

Father, I love that Your will for me is to rejoice! And to pray to You. And to thank You for everything. What a wonderful will for my life! This world is so negative and can drag me down. But You, Lord, intend to bring life. You want me to live a life that overflows with joy. When I have bad days, help me turn to You in prayer. Even when it feels like things are crumbling around me, I pray I'll be able to find something worth thanking You for—something I can rejoice over. Please help me focus on the wonderful things that are happening even tonight. I want to experience the true freedom that comes through You. In Jesus' name I pray, amen.

Think about it!
What wonderful things are you thankful for tonight?

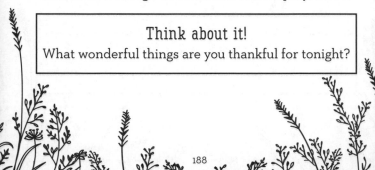

FORGETTING WHAT'S BEHIND

Brothers, I do not consider that I have made it my own. But one thing I do: forgetting what lies behind and straining forward to what lies ahead, I press on toward the goal for the prize of the upward call of God in Christ Jesus.

PHILIPPIANS 3:13–14 ESV

Lord Jesus, as I've trusted You with my life and believe that You are my living Savior, You've promised me an eternity with You! A reward instead of punishment. Life with You instead of separation. A transformed heart and soul. Help me to forget about the things of this world. I pray I won't get bogged down with everyday matters. I pray I'll forget the past. Instead, I want to press on to live in Your freedom for all my tomorrows. You've called me to an amazing prize—I pray I might strain toward that every day, remembering You're my Lord and that You've called me Your own. In Your name I pray, amen.

Think about it!
Should we worry about yesterday or, instead, focus on tomorrow?

ALL I NEED

Whom have I in heaven but you? And there
is nothing on earth that I desire besides you.
My flesh and my heart may fail, but God is the
strength of my heart and my portion forever.
PSALM 73:25–26 ESV

Father, You are all I want. There's nothing else on this earth I truly desire except for You. Everyday things and people try to rob my attention and affection from You; but in my very core, I know nothing else compares to You. No other relationship. No possession. No award or honor or opportunity. You and You alone are the true strength of my heart. Everything and everyone else might fall away, but I'll still have You. Please keep my focus on You, Lord. Thank You for being my one true, steady, never-failing rock who I can base my life, future, and eternity on. In Jesus' name I pray, amen.

Think about it!
When it comes down to it, what do you *really* need?

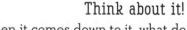

SO MUCH LIFE

*"I came that they may have life,
and have it abundantly."*
JOHN 10:10 NASB

Father, You are the giver of all life. You are the Creator of life; and Jesus came so that I might live an abundant life. Some days my life doesn't feel so amazing, though. It's easy to become discouraged, and sometimes I don't even want to face what tomorrow might bring. I pray that You would open my eyes to see the gift of life. Please help me see how important I am in the lives of other people. And please, even (and especially) when I'm feeling down, show me how I can use my life for You. Protect me from Satan's schemes to steal, kill, and destroy. Please help me live for You! In Jesus' name I pray, amen.

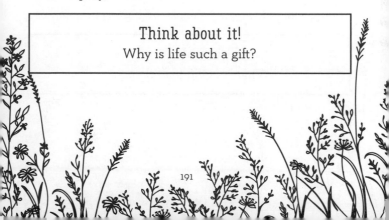

Think about it!
Why is life such a gift?

LISTEN

*The Lord GOD has given me the tongue of
those who are taught, that I may know how
to sustain with a word him who is weary.
Morning by morning he awakens; he awakens
my ear to hear as those who are taught.*

ISAIAH 50:4 ESV

Lord, I want You to lead me; and I want to follow Your lead. Sometimes, though, I get confused about what You want from me. Tomorrow morning, could You please make it clear? Please help me focus on You and Your truth. When I'm feeling weary with all of the things I need to do, please refresh me. I want to learn to rest in You and listen to You throughout each day. I believe You will reveal Your will and Word to me. Thank You for always being there for me and always being willing to guide me. In Jesus' name I pray, amen.

> ## Think about it!
> Where is God leading you?

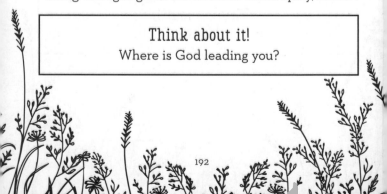